Arts & Crafts for Children

THE WORLD BOOK OF

Arts & Crafts for Children

Arnold Arnold

M

ISBN o 333 21295 9

First published in Great Britain 1976 by
Macmillan London Limited
London and Basingstoke
Associated companies in New York, Toronto,
Dublin, Melbourne, Johannesburg and Delhi

Reprinted 1977

First published in the U.S.A. 1975 by
Thomas Y. Crowell Company
Published simultaneously in Canada by
Fitzhenry and Whiteside Limited

Printed in Great Britain by Billing & Sons Ltd.
British Library Cataloguing in Publication Data
Arnold, Arnold
  The world book of arts and crafts for
  children.
  Index.
  ISBN 0-333-21295-9
  1. Title
  745.5'02'4054 TT157
  Handicraft

To all children and especially to my own:
Geoffrey, Marguerite and Francis;
To the child within me;
To Gail;
And to the future

Contents

Foreword

Children learn best through play. They develop and hone skills by experimenting with materials, tools and their own unfolding capacities. But they also need guidance. They don't acquire good learning habits by being drilled, by being forced to copy or learn by rote, or by being shown how to 'produce'. These principles have long been accepted by enlightened British educators, and they have recently been reaffirmed by both Plowden and Bullock Reports.

Many secondary schools do offer art, craft and design courses. But they are optional and, above infant-school levels, reserved for the non-academic student. Indeed, it is possible to take 'O' and 'A' levels in ceramics and art, though it is patently absurd to test a fifteen- or eighteen-year-old's performance in art or craft. While these tests seem to lend a spurious respectability to the arts, they also turn them into yet another credentials-acquisition ploy.

This book is intended for all children and not just for those who demonstrate special aptitude for or interest in art or craft. Moreover, I hope to influence parents and teachers to encourage the children in their charge to use tools and materials in an inventive manner. All children need some of these experiences, at home and in school.

Historically, craftsmanship declines in proportion to industrialization. This is true for all cultures. Esquimaux who live in Quonset huts lose their igloo-building skills. They also lose an important part of their cultural heritage. This is unavoidable to some extent. But the decultured Esquimaux lose out on other scores. They become confused, neurotic and dissatisfied, without knowing why. They lose their will to work and survive. Many become perpetual welfare clients. Eventually they become extinct.

Signs of cultural decline and disorientation are visible throughout the technologically developed world. More than the current economic crisis, Britain, like other industrialized nations, suffers a psychological one that is linked to a loss in skills and craftsmanship. Until very recently, Britain was one of the most craft-conscious countries in the world. British craftsmanship was legendary, even in industry. British goods were sought everywhere. British craftsmanship extended to the factory floor, the office and even to the retail shop. Pride of craft may seem like an absurdity now, but it enhances the self-esteem and work satisfaction of everyone. The quality of and demand for British goods have declined correspondingly. The effect on individuals is not merely economic. Most Britons no longer take pride in acquiring and practising skills, and the products of their labour fail to satisfy them and their customers. No amount of North Sea oil will restore this loss.

A return to craft-consciousness offers Britain one avenue of national, cultural and spiritual revival. Britain can only compete with countries more lavishly endowed with raw materials, space and automation by a return to craftsmanship. Such a revival requires an education of present-day and future generations in all walks of life – managers, factory workers, individual creators, government bureaucrats, teachers and students – who are experienced in and have respect for artistry and craftsmanship. The industries of the future that will allow Britain to thrive once again can find their beginnings only in a revival of creative craftsmanship.

A return to craft-consciousness, especially in the education of children, will pay rich dividends in the quality of individual, family and community life. It builds character, endurance and self-reliance among young and old. The traditions of such craftsmanship have deep roots in Britain. They need merely be reinterpreted to serve modern requirements. The British eighteenth-century family relied largely on crafts practised by all its members. Victorian homes of all classes were partially handmade. John Ruskin and William Morris a hundred years ago, and Sir Herbert Read in this century, foresaw the consequences of the decline in British craftsmanship. These men may seem dated and romantic dreamers today, but they were prophetic. I should like this book to make the educational and creative opportunities that were once the privilege of the few available to all children. They need and deserve them.

Arnold Arnold, London, 1976

1 Approaches and attitudes

... They have no pleasure in the work by which they make their bread ... for they feel that the kind of labour to which they are condemned is verily a degrading one, and makes them less than men. *John Ruskin*

'Evidence of non-involvement and the disinclination to exert effort are appearing in homes and classrooms . . . What does this behaviour mean? . . . What is today's environment feeding back to children? All around, children see adults place greater reliance on mechanical aids than on their own capacities and resources.'* Written by an astute teacher and observer of children, this is a terrible indictment of our times and attitudes. But what can we expect? We plonk children before the TV set at earliest ages from three to seven hours

each day. Here processes, skills and achievements are necessarily telescoped. Anything portrayed on TV looks as if it could be done by anyone without experience and with a very small expenditure of time, effort and devotion. Small wonder that children's endurance and respect for excellence are eroded.

This book offers concerned parents, teachers, recreation workers and therapists the means to counteract these trends.

Children need values and ethics. Our society fails them in these respects more than in any other. Art and craft provide opportunities for awakening practical senses of right and wrong, what works and what doesn't, what is permissible and possible and what isn't, and an ability to savour success and cope with momentary failure and frustration. They foster

* Dorothy H. Cohen, 'Children of Technology: Images or The Real Thing' in *Childhood Education*, J. of The Association for Childhood Education International, Washington, DC, 48:6:3.72, 298–300

making judgements. Every stroke of hammer or brush is a decision. The child learns in art and craft activities to consider each such decision in advance and to live with the result. We can't afford to allow our children's creative abilities and endowments to atrophy in expectation that they won't need these in an expected technological future. Its promised benefits have proven elusive. The earth cannot support ever-expanding population growth. The technologies have polluted the environment, concentrated non-absorbable wastes on land and in the sea and air, and are making life hazardous and unhealthy. 'Only madmen and economists believe growth can go on for ever in a finite world.'*

Nature inevitably redresses such imbalances if it can. And so the choice is a return to a labour-intensive husbandry of resources, or disaster. Implicit in either course is the exercise of craft by those who wish to prosper and survive – the change in life style or a possible ecological debacle. It is with hope for the former rather than fear of calamity that this book has been written. Genuine craft attitudes are a vital necessity if our children are to have the means to thrive during the difficult

* Jeremy Swift, *The Other Eden*: Dent, 1974

decades ahead. Art can endow them with beauty and purpose. The practice of both will assure that essential human qualities will be preserved and enhanced, come what may.

The background material that precedes each of the following chapters suggests attitudes for introducing art and craft techniques to children and young people. One without the other has no value. I therefore hope that these introductions are read with as much care and attention as the recipes.

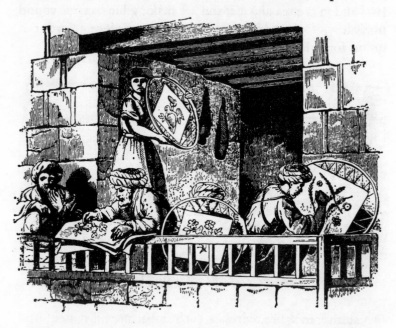

There are two reasons for educating children. The first is, or should be, to elicit and develop their humanity. The second is to make them economically independent and useful. In automating production, and training young people for work in such an economy, we tend to lose sight of the first, essential object of learning: the exercise of species specific skills, irrespective of their economic usefulness.

Many of our schools neglect manual education at primary

and secondary levels as the demand for genuine craft declines. This has caused a deterioration in general competence and also in the consumer's judgement. It creates 'a mechanization of responsibility as well, taking judgement farther and farther away from the minds, and therefore the ethics, of men'.*

Education in essential human skills is likely to decline further as it has already in fields in which automation has taken command – in printing and tool- and die-making trades, for example. Humanness may die piecemeal. And unless this trend is reversed at least in so far as the education of young people is concerned, we may need a redefinition of what it means to be human.

Significantly, there has been a strong revival of arts and crafts, especially among the disaffected young. Unfortunately, many who engage in craft occupations as young adults or who practise them for the first time as hobbies in middle or old age suffer a distorted creative sense imposed by miseducation and misinformation. Even when they use tools, they don't exercise craft. 'The housewife who bakes her own bread according to a recipe, sews a dress from a pattern [that she did not design] . . . is doing useful, satisfying, but contrary to the women's magazines, uncreative work . . . To do by hand what a machine ordinarily does is not a creative act.'†

Most art and craft manuals, instruction books, periodicals, kits and even teachers stress production, following or tracing patterns, plans and recipes. This is a denial of the very essence of creative tool use. It is essential that children should be sheltered from such production in early as much as in later years. They need exposure to the creative processes of art and craft.

* Ward Just, *Military Men*: Avon Books, 1970
† Judith Groch, *The Right to Create*: Little, Brown & Co, 1969

1 Art and craft education

Where schools, museums and other institutions fail children, it is up to parents to make up the deficit. Proper introduction to the arts and crafts affects a child's personality, outlook, achievement and future, regardless of his individual bent or eventual career. It refines abilities, no matter which stream of higher education, vocation or avocation he or she enters later. A young man or woman who enjoys a background and interest in any of the arts or crafts will be more sensitive to people, ideas and the material world. He or she will be able to choose, care for, value and use the tools of his or her calling and those required for daily existence with discretion and imagination. And he or she will certainly be more likely to survive successfully in a declining world economy than those who cannot use their hands.

The increase in leisure and the nature of employment today make art and craft education a necessity. For the moment at least a large part of the population in technologically developed countries spends more time in leisure than on life-supporting labour. Our children need skills that will sustain their interests in adulthood during their hours and years away from work. Those lacking avocational interests tend to become passive; their abilities atrophy; they lack lustre and curiosity; they are frustrated and dissatisfied; and their life expectancy is shortened. Genuine craft – and not do-it-yourself projects – could engage and satisfy them. But this requires an education in childhood and youth that stresses creative development.

The art and craft education of children requires more than mere exposure to tools and materials. Children need direct contacts with active artists and craftsmen. They need to see them work in the flesh and be able to touch their work. They need a familiarity with different styles and forms created in former times and in different cultures, as well as in their own, not to imitate, but to be inspired by them.

2 Ages and stages

Young children can be introduced to a great variety of tools and materials, provided elementary safety precautions and what the child can and cannot yet do are kept in mind. For example, any five-year-old, who has built with blocks, drawn, painted and finger-painted, can handle a coping saw or jigsaw into which a spiral safety blade has been inserted. But first the child needs direction. He must be provided with a proper workspace, with tools and materials. He needs incentives and to have the nature of the work pointed out to him. This is true at all stages of development. It is equally important to shelter today's child from the temptation to imitate TV, comic book, cartoon and other pervasive stereotypes, encouraging him to invent his own symbols.

3 Individual differences

Not every child is equally inventive or inclined to identical interests. Some prefer to draw, others to sculpt; still others enjoy work with wood, leather, fibres, fabric or film. A child can learn identical skills from any art and equal satisfaction in craft. All provide opportunities for expression and development of self, provided they are introduced in a proper manner.

Every child enjoys working with his or her hands. His or her inclinations are most readily observable at early ages before they are overlaid by outside influences. But you can only discover and nurture them by exposure to direct experience with tools and materials. A child's interest in any art or craft can also serve as a focal point for other learning, including academic skills. One who doesn't read with interest or skill may suddenly become passionately immersed in books dealing with a craft subject that engages him. Another, who may be uninterested in numbers, will discover that mathematics has practical uses in making plans, or measuring or weighing the materials with which he enjoys working.

4 Special children

Conventional definitions of intelligence are extremely limited and inexact. Children are quite often classified as mentally retarded, hyperactive, autistic, slow learners or even brain-damaged when their abilities lie outside what is usually taught and tested. Art and craft education offers parents, teachers and therapists alternative opportunities for reaching many children and young people who are otherwise neglected or left behind in the classroom.

5 Process versus production

A misunderstanding of the difference between learning and performance has created confusion in the art and craft education of children as in most other aspects of education. *Production* is not, and should not be, the object of manual skill development and self-expression. Instead, it can and should lead to the discovery of *processes*.

Creative work involves a progressive discovery of tools, materials, processes and self, and how they can be transformed imaginatively. Such creation may be frustrating or exhilarating or both. It may lead to messes or masterpieces. None of this is important to the child, except in so far as it leads to exercise, experience, new insights, competence, independence, co-ordination, wonder, curiosity, intuition, spontaneity, whimsy, discovery, self-discipline and endurance. Most of these qualities are not measured or measurable. They are especially important because few schools stimulate and none can test them.

A child given colouring books and 'paint-by-number' kits can turn out Mona Lisas or Last Suppers on an assembly line.

One who is reared on 'hobby kits' can produce a stream of miniature ballistic missiles and detailed facsimile space capsules merely by gluing bits of prefabricated plastic together. This kind of mass production is mesmerizing and habit-forming. It fosters an illusion of craft and creativity. Such activities are only unskilled, menial and soul-destroying labour.

But a child who slowly builds competence by daubing clumsily with a paintbrush discovers how to bend materials to his will. A child who is experienced in such craft becomes progressively critical of his own efforts.

Ultimately the child's creation does turn into a product of some sort. 'What shall I make?' is not an unreasonable question for a child to ask once he has mastered new tools and skills. Or he may be inspired to learn because he wants to make or invent something, draw, paint or sculpt what he experiences or feels, or build an object he wants to use in play or give as a present. Or he may simply wish to make his surroundings more beautiful. Especially then his work should not evade the creative processes of art and craft. It should be self-generated and not depend on prefabricated parts, patterns or plans.

6 Play, self-expression and creativity

Play, self-expression, creativity and art are usually inexactly and loosely defined. The following describes what is meant by these terms for the purposes of this book.

Child's play differs from that of most adults because personality, abilities and intellect are in formative stages during childhood. The child literally 'forms' himself through play.* It is his work and means to growth. The adult 're-forms'

* Judy Ann Spitler, 'Changing View of Play in the Education of Young Children': Teachers College, Columbia University, 1971 (PhD thesis, unpublished)

himself by the same process. For most it is recreation. But the quality of *playfulness* is common to both adult and child. Such playfulness is the essence of *self-expression* and *creativity* and it serves as the most useful definition of these hackneyed terms.

Craft describes the exercise of skills. It is the hallmark of competence. An artist practises craft when he paints or sculpts. A scientist practises craft when he prepares a slide for his microscope. A mechanic practises craft when he repairs a car. None of these acts is creative unless an element of inventive playfulness enters into the manipulation of tools and materials. The degree to which a child may depart from prescribed paths in his self-expressive play decides the extent to which he can create himself.

Art involves the playful use of self. This is why children are creative by definition. But by definition they also lack experience, competence and craft. Children need tools and materials presented to them in a way that allows them to discover their disciplined uses. Craft can accomplish this only if it is introduced as a process rather than as a means of production. Without playfulness the child turns into a mindless producer. Without craft he lacks the means to achieve mature playfulness. And he can only acquire the former through the exercise of the latter.

7 What to teach and when

The judgement of what to teach – and when not to teach – emerges when art and craft are viewed as educational processes. The decision of what to do, make or express must be left to the child once he sets to work. First, however, work space, tools and materials must be provided. The desirable balance between direction and freedom can be achieved only 'if the teacher [or parent] is one who inspires rather than dictates, where the discoveries about the nature of materials are discussed so that children learn through [their own and] each other's experience as well as from the teacher. A group of ten-year-olds, for example, might discover that wax crayons resist water-based ink. From this starting point [simple wax-resist] the gifted teacher will try to create situations in which the process of using wax to repel water is examined in as many contrasting ways as possible.'*

A child can learn the limits of safety and behaviour in art and craft as in all other activities. He needs to discover how to arrange, control and care for his tools. He must understand that he may not paint on the wall or decorate baby brother's hair with clay. He needs to be shown the disciplines of craft, while the playful and experimental aspects of art must be left in his hands.

Every beginner in art and craft – adult, teenager or child – tends to lose control over his medium. The materials spread as if they had a will of their own, from the centre of the table to its edges and beyond. Things are spilled, surfaces marred, and an object that is the product of hours of thoughtful labour is shattered in the confusion.

You can show the child that things work better if he keeps materials in bins and boxes, hangs up his tools in prearranged places when they aren't in use, and keeps them in good working order. He needs clothing, table and floor spaces that are washable. How hammer or coping saw must be held and how to nail or drill to best effect and in safety must be demonstrated. The child needs properly organized material and tool storage places. He needs help with cleaning up messes until he can be expected to do this unaided. But don't expect too much, too soon, from a child. Ceaseless demand for self-discipline and neatness can be as discouraging as constant disorder.

* Henry Pluckrose, quoted in *The Fourth R: A Commentary on Youth, Education, and the Arts* by Joseph Featherstone: Associated Council of the Arts, 1972

The visual, auditory and tactile qualities of materials must be pointed out to the child. He needs to learn how to recognize and identify them and how to express them verbally and in his creative work. Experience and familiarity with the origins of material will increase his interest in them. Eventually he will want to know how to weigh and measure, plan and design when projects demand precision. But even these skills

evolve from spontaneous experiences that lead from non-numerical to geometric and eventually to numerical judgements.

Parents and teachers should work with craft materials themselves and become familiar with the opportunities they offer. But in presenting the same materials to children, parents and teachers must remember the developmental level of each child and of his or her previous experiences. In any event don't show the child tricks – how to draw in perspective, in proportion, or a 'stick' man. Children can only see and express things one-dimensionally until they reach quite advanced stages of development.* But this can never be accelerated. Interference can short-circuit it.

8 Tools, materials and judgement

Children and young people can only discover the allowable limits of the technologies through an education in manual arts and crafts. This does not suggest a return to hand labour for the sake of misplaced nostalgia.

Since the advent of industrialization and with the explosion of the technologies, tools have proliferated to an extent that most have escaped ethical governance. As a result, we lack principles required to guide us in their use, from steam to internal combustion engine, from chemicals, drugs and plastics to nuclear energy.

These are persuasive reasons for educating children and young people in handicrafts. A wooden plank cut up with a handsaw teaches a child more than the gift of a factory-made box, ready for decoration. A fabric remnant that the child cuts, glues, staples or sews to form an abstract design or an ill-fitting doll's apron provides more valuable experiences than a gift of patterns that assure a perfect result, or a whole wardrobe of Barbie-doll dresses. It is infinitely more productive if a child improvises a paper, cardboard or twig loom than if he weaves on a miniature, prefabricated and prestrung one. These suggestions are not made for the sake of economy but for the sake of the child.

9 Mixed media, skills and scrap materials

Once a child has learned how to handle a hand drill and how to choose the right bit for making a hole in a particular material, he can apply the same skill and knowledge to wood,

* Arnold Arnold, *Teaching Your Child to Learn from Birth to School Age*: Prentice-Hall, 1971

metal, brick or seashells for that matter. He should be encouraged to look for and find a variety of materials on which to exercise his skills, tools, and imagination, rather than limiting himself to one application. Experience with and especially the discovery of a variety of raw, manufactured and scrap materials enable the young craftsman to draw on and choose from a large reservoir of different media. He'll use the proper tool required for each different material because he is sensitive to their differences in texture, density and weight. He can shape any material to achieve a desired effect. These abilities are necessary for life in a world rich with diverse materials and experiences.

The search for diversity in effect and for possible combinations of different materials is a creative act in itself. It brings harmony to what, on the surface, may seem like clashing or divergent characteristics. A large part of the art consists of discovering how each can support, complement or counteract all others. This is why collages and assemblages are stressed in many of the following chapters. They are not 'modern' art; they are essential experiences. Abstraction underlies the work of even traditional and realistic artists and craftsmen. It is also the structure that underlies a child's later outlook, as in creation. He learns to see, recognize and create structure, instead of being confused by surface detail. And so the assemblage the child makes out of scraps of paper and wood enables him eventually to get greater satisfaction out of his still or movie camera than if he lacked this experience.

10 Work spaces, lighting and clothing
(See also 81, 113 and 138.)

A child does not need a carpenter's bench for work with wood any more than he needs an easel for painting. He does need a solid worktable for either, large and low enough so that he can work in comfort, sitting or standing. A well-built trestle table can serve the purpose (see diagram). It should consist of a 2-cm ($\frac{3}{4}$-inch) plywood top, with all surfaces carefully sanded and coated with several light applications of varnish or shellac. Sawhorses make practical legs provided the tabletop is attached to them firmly. A child outgrows other worktables rapidly. Metal sawhorse angle brackets can be bought inexpensively in any hardware shop. 2·5cm × 5cm (1″ × 2″) wooden legs can be inserted into these and replaced with

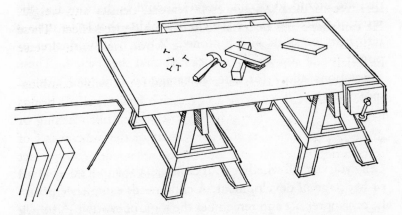

longer ones as the child grows taller. 2·5cm × 5cm (1″ × 2″) strips should be glued and screwed also to the underside of the tabletop so that it cannot slide off the sawhorses as the child works (see diagram).

Either trestle table or tabletop carpenter's workbench can be used for any kind of art or craft work. A woodworking vice (see 91) can be attached. Wooden rails can be nailed or screwed in place to secure small parts, bins, tools and paint jars. A pegboard, hung within reach, can become a tool storage centre.

Shelves and receptacles are required for materials storage. The floor under and around the worktable should be protected.

The worktable or bench should be placed next to a window so that the light falls on the work from the side opposite the child's handedness (from the left for a right-handed child, and from the right for a left-handed child). He should not face, nor should his back be turned to, the window while he works. An overhead light is needed for work after dark or on overcast days, so that work spaces are relatively shadow-free. Keep extension cords out of the way, out from underfoot, and out of the child's reach.

A smock or old clothing will protect the child from spills that are bound to occur. Sleeves should be buttoned at the wrist or rolled up above the elbows. Shirts should be tucked into belts or skirts and buttoned. When heat-producing or power tools are used, smocks should be belted. These suggestions allow for safe, unhampered limb and manual movements.

11 Safety

Only you can tell whether your child can use a tool safely at his or her stage of development. A child needs experience before he can appreciate and remember the logic of caution. A totally protected and inexperienced child is far more likely to injure himself and others than one who is gradually exposed to experiences, including those that pose minor hazards, provided he receives guidance and supervision. Children usually confine themselves to working with tools on appropriate materials *if these are furnished*. A hammer given without tacks or wood invariably invites inappropriate use. Insisting that a child follows given patterns and plans also leads to potentially damaging experimentation when no one is looking. The gift of new tools must coincide with a time at which the child understands what he may and may not do with them. You must become aware of hazards, and foresee and point them out as often and as patiently as necessary. Do not expect a child, even at ages when he or she can read, to study and heed the cautions on labels or packages. You must do this yourself and then make appropriate judgements about the possible dangers.

Proper arrangement of the child's work spaces (see 10), when and how materials are introduced, and foresight will prevent accidents. All tools and materials suggested in this book are safe if given as and when recommended, with some exceptions for which special cautions are listed in every case. Your attention is drawn to those tools and materials that are sharp, pointed or potentially toxic in the hands of children too immature to use them with caution.

Two materials – plastics and glass – are largely excluded from this book for safety reasons. Plastic scrap, like vinyl, can be glued to collages and assemblages without danger, provided organic glues are used, but such scraps will not adhere permanently.

Virtually all synthetic paints and glues, except acrylics, and all aerosol spray paints and adhesives are highly toxic and potentially carcinogenic. Some synthetic glues bond so effectively that any of the material that dries on the skin, or a part accidentally glued to a finger, may require surgery for removal. Many tar- and cellulose-derived finishes and glues, as well as paints, dyes and ceramic glazes that contain lead, are dangerous and inappropriate for use by young people. (See also 165.)

12 Organization of contents

Each of the chapters in this book deals with one major craft, art or materials subject, and is subdivided into parts in an ascending order of skill and difficulty. General background or cautionary information is given within these subdivisions. The number of art and craft projects themselves, and the amount of subject matter included, are possible only because duplication is avoided through cross-references. For example, cutting with scissors requires the same basic instructions and cautions whether the material is paper, foil, cloth or thin, split leather. Overlapping skills are described only once, in appropriate places, and cross-referenced by section-number whenever the same technique applies elsewhere.

2 Paper and foil

We need craftsmanship in education, in a machine age as much,
if not more than any other, because it is a fundamental *mode of
education*, through which the child explores, discovers the
qualities of, and comes to terms with the world in which he
lives. *Mairi Seonaid Robertson*

13 Background

Paper was first invented in China by Ts'ai Lun in the year
AD105. It was made of the bark of the mulberry bush, similar
to tapa cloth still used by Pacific islanders. By the time of
Marco Polo paper was made in the Far East by pressing
vegetable fibres into sheets in a manner not very different from
modern techniques. Paper objects and miniatures were also

used in religious ceremonies. Foil-covered paper money was a part of Chinese funerary rites as early as AD739.

The ancient Egyptians used the leaves of the papyrus tree – hence our word 'paper' – pasted into sheets for record-keeping. The Romans discovered how to make parchment – sheepskin sliced very thin. This remained the sole writing surface throughout Europe for many centuries. England's first paper

making factory was established in 1495 but failed almost immediately due to a lack of demand. A second, similar venture was started in 1586. It thrived as a result of Gutenberg's invention of movable type some fifty years earlier (see 202). Paper making remained a laborious process until the nineteenth century and the invention of power-driven machinery. The basic raw materials and processes – vegetable and cloth fibres; wood pulp; clay and chemicals added for different weights, textures and colours, laid on to a variety of screens and then dried and pressed, washed and bleached – remained virtually the same. More recently plastics have been introduced to paper and paperboard making. Yet a few craftsmen still produce handmade papers for special purposes.

In China, Japan, Korea and India children have enjoyed a profusion of paper and papier mâché toys and paper folding, pasting and related craft for centuries. Many, like origami, are traditional by now and children develop skill, patience and a quality of mind peculiar to the culture of childhood in the Orient. Until the late eighteenth century paper did not fall into the hands of European children, save for occasional waste scraps. But from about 1800 onwards it became an important raw material of play and for the production of kites, balloons, toy soldiers and doll and structural cutouts, among other playthings.

First projects
14 Crumpling, twisting and tearing
Tools and materials: coloured tissue paper; bond paper; newspaper

Crumpling paper, rolling it into balls, twisting it into sausages, or simply tearing it to shreds can be extremely satisfying to a young child. It calls different sensations and muscles into play. The child discovers textures and other properties of the material. Tissue and other paper balls can be strung, taped or pasted together; or, tied to twine, can be dragged by a toddler behind him.

Place the child before a table at which he can work in comfort (see 10) or in his highchair. Give him an assortment of paper and a large, empty box. Then show him how to crumple, twist and tear and put the pieces into the box. (See also 207.)

15 Sorting
Tools and materials: same as 14; empty egg carton or assortment of small boxes

Once a child enjoys crumpling, twisting and tearing paper, he can be shown how to sort the different pieces. Set him up with an empty egg carton or a number of small boxes or containers.

Demonstrate how he can distribute the shapes he creates, sorting them by relative size, shape or colour. Aside from sheer play value, this sets the stage for size, shape and colour recognition, and sorting and labelling skills and controls that are necessary for other learning.

16 Wrapping

Tools and materials: tissue paper; newspaper; small paper bags; small empty boxes; toys and other objects; 1·25cm ($\frac{1}{2}$″) masking tape cut into 2·5cm (1″) strips, each taped to the edge of the tabletop by one corner

Unwrapping presents is one of the joys of childhood. Wrapping things up can give a child similar pleasure. Wrapping a box and making it 'disappear' is a kind of magic. Quite incidentally the child discovers how to fold paper and tape down corners, edges and folds.

NOTE Do not give young children plastic bags or cellophane tape. The first can be hazardous and the second frustrating.

Lacing
17 Making a threader

Tools and materials: drinking straws cut into 2·5cm (1″) lengths; white paste (see 21 and 23–5); strands of coloured-wool yarn

Before a child learns to lace he can be shown how to make his own threader. Choose lengths of yarn long enough for whatever is to be laced or strung.

It takes nearly 130cm (50″) of yarn to lace round the edges of a perforated piece of 21·6cm × 27·9cm (8$\frac{1}{2}$″ × 11″) bond paper. Dip about 1cm ($\frac{1}{2}$″) of one end of the yarn into the paste and twirl it between thumb and forefinger to point the tip. Insert this end into one of the straw cut-offs while the paste is still wet and let it dry thoroughly. Tie a thick knot into the other end of the yarn, and the child is ready to string beads and macaroni shapes, or to lace punched paper (see 18). A blunt lacing needle, used in leather craft (see 127), is also a good, safe tool for young children. Plastic- or metal-tipped shoe laces are usually too short and not nearly as colourful.

18 Punching holes

Tools and materials: paper hole punch (see 126 for revolving punch); assorted white and coloured construction and bond papers; foil; paper cups and plates; threader (see 17)

A child old enough to thread and lace may not have the strength to use a hole punch. This may have to be done for him at first. Punch holes at regular or irregular intervals around the edges of the paper. Holes can be punched into inside areas by folding the paper one or more times (see

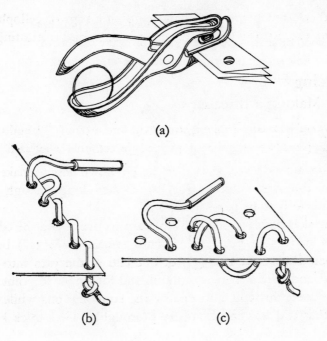

(a)

(b)   (c)

diagram a). Show the child how to insert his threader at whichever hole he chooses, pulling the yarn all the way through to the knotted end. Demonstrate how he can lace over and under (see diagram b) or bind the edges (see diagram c), always pulling the spare yarn all the way through each hole at every turn. He'll discover the variety of patterns he can create going from one hole to the next, skipping some and criss-crossing in every direction. Prepare several straw-tipped threaders in advance so that he can work with concentration until he tires.

Eventually the child will be able to punch his or her own holes. Save the punched-out paper discs for use in pasting (see 21), collages (see 29) and paper mosaics (see 31).

19 Grommet lacing

Tools and materials: grommet and die set (available in needlework shops) (see also 130); child-size hammer (see 84); 30cm × 30cm × 2cm (12″ × 12″ × ¾″) well-sanded pine board, plywood or scrap wood, or a sheet of heavy cardboard; paper hole punch (see 18); threader (see 17); paper products (see 18)

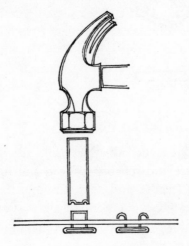

After the holes have been punched as in 18 above, tape one edge of the paper to the wooden board and show the child how to push one grommet up through one of the holes. Use the grommet die and hammer to demonstrate how to bend the rim of the grommet so that it is securely fastened to the paper (see diagram). Make sure that the threader fits through the grommet. When the child has finished attaching all the grommets, he can lace and unlace his designs since the grommets strengthen the paper holes so that they won't tear.

20 Lacing cut paper shapes together

Tools and materials: same as 17 and 18; scissors (see 38)

Small paper shapes – circles, squares, triangles, rectangles and irregularly shaped pieces – can be laced, one to all others, if holes have been punched into each. Once a child is able to handle child-size scissors (see 38–40), he can cut out his own paper shapes for lacing.

Pasting and gluing
21 First steps in pasting

Ordinary white school paste, casein-based glues, mucilage and acrylics are water soluble and harmless if swallowed. Do not give pre-school and junior-school children other adhesives, cow gum or epoxy (see 11 and 165). (See 23–7 for homemade paste and glue recipes.)

22 Adhesives for older children

Use organic and acrylic adhesives only, until the child is sufficiently mature and reliable to heed and follow cautions and instructions (see 11 and 165). Children have accidents, even at older ages. They are not likely to wash their hands as often or as well as they should after handling glues that might be toxic. Cow gum, like aeroplane dope and other adhesives commonly used by young people, is toxic and inflammable.

23 Making your own adhesives

The following glues can be made easily and require only materials that are found in any home or local shops. They keep well in the refrigerator or other cool place in closed, screw-top jars. If the glue becomes too stiff to use or dries out, it can be restored by the addition of a little water. All except one of the recipes (see 26) are entirely non-toxic, and many are useful for paper as well as for bonding other materials, as detailed in each instance.

24 Flour paste (short-term adhesion)

Tools and materials: flour; water; mixing bowl

Mixed to a consistency of double cream, this is a useful adhesive for paper, cloth and other materials. It is not permanent but the adhesion will last long enough for most pre-schoolers' and infants' purposes.

25 Flour paste (long-term adhesion)

Tools and materials: flour; water; muslin or cheesecloth; glass dish

Wrap a handful of flour in the muslin. Wash and knead the flour inside the muslin bag under cold, running water until the water is no longer milky as it runs off and most of the starch is removed. The remainder is almost pure gluten. Allow to dry in a glass dish. The dry gluten will store indefinitely without refrigeration.

To use, chip flakes off the gluten cake, add a few drops of cold water, and allow to stand for a few minutes. Then knead the flakes until they become soft and pliant. Add more cold water to thin out to the required consistency.

26 Transparent glue

Tools and materials: 25g (2oz) white gelatine; 150g (5oz) acetic acid (available at chemist's); 175g (6oz) water; cooking pot

Soak gelatine in water for twelve hours. Then heat the softened gelatine in the same water until it dissolves. Stir in acetic acid and add cold water until the mixture comes to about half a litre (one pint).

This glue is slightly toxic, but strong enough to cement glass. It can be made stronger or weaker by using more or less gelatine. An older child can use it to mount photographs, pictures cut from magazines, or his own drawings on paper, wood or glass. By brushing the adhesive on top of the pictures as well as coating them on the reverse side, they will adhere and be protected at the same time. Wipe off any excess before the glue sets with a cloth soaked in warm water.

27 Cornflour paste

Tools and materials: 2 tablespoons cornflour; ¼ teaspoon alum; 1 cup water; oil of cloves; cooking pot

Mix flour, alum and part of the water to form a smooth cream. Add the balance of the water, stir, and cook over low heat until the mixture becomes translucent. The longer it cooks, the greater the adhesive power. Add a few drops of oil of cloves after the mixture is taken off the stove. Keep in closed jar in the refrigerator and stir thoroughly before using. This is a useful adhesive for paper, cloth, wood and thin leather especially.

28 Acrylic adhesives

Acrylic media are a relatively recent development. They are available from art supply stores and school material suppliers. The painting medium itself is water soluble and non-toxic and can be used as an adhesive and, at the same time, as an opaque or transparent varnish and protective coating. When totally dry, it waterproofs whatever it covers. Acrylics are therefore ideal adhesives for collages (see 29) and assemblages (see 30), and as varnish for papier mâché (see 47–57), painting (see 148–71) and sculpting (see 195–9).

29 Collages

Tools and materials: paste or glue (see 21–8);
empty egg cartons or small boxes; scrap materials;
sheets of white card; drawing paper; brown wrapping paper;
cardboard; bowl with wide base, filled with water; sponge or rags

Keep glue, water and other materials to one side of a newspaper-covered table, depending on the child's 'handedness' (see 10). Let the child sort the different scrap materials by kind, shape or colour in the egg cartons or other small containers. Then suggest that he arranges and pastes the materials down on the paper or cardboard. Once started, a child will think of ingenious and original ways of combining the materials.

Demonstrate working methods – how to apply a little glue at a time; how to brush it on; and how to keep the jar closed to prevent the glue drying out. Point out the contrasting qualities and textures of the materials. Name colours and shapes and assist – but don't do all the work – in cleaning up. Don't show the child how to make pictures or designs.

Praise inventiveness, good work habits, and endurance. Don't compare his creations with those produced by other children or by adults, or with reality. Display the child's work.

Comment on unique features of his conceptions. Restrict your suggestions to those that will help him achieve what he wants to make in an effective, organized manner.

Ordinary newspaper can be similarly cut up and pasted together again so that different patterns of type and portions of photographs are re-formed into unique designs. A child can draw or paint into his collage, cut up and use his own drawings, and combine them with scrap and other materials in decorative ways.

30 Assemblages

Tools and materials: scrap materials; paste or glue (see 21–8); wire (see 116–18); wood, plywood or heavy cardboard base

Assemblages are three-dimensional collages. They can be constructed on or around a wood or cardboard base or free-standing wood, wire or cardboard forms or frames to which other materials are adhered. These can be pasted, nailed, screwed, bolted or worked on, depending on the availability of materials and tools and the child's level of skill development. Portions can be painted, shellacked or varnished, and the finished assemblage may stand free, or hang on a wall or from an overhead fixture.

31 Paper mosaics

Tools and materials: shallow jewellery or shoebox lid; or picture frame or moulding nailed or glued to a wood or cardboard base; paste (see 21–8); seeds; beans; peas; macaroni shapes; seashells; snippets of white or coloured paper; punched-out paper (see 18) and other small or cut-apart scrap materials

A mosaic can be a kind of collage of small, more or less uniform or dissimilar, multicoloured or monochromatic snippets of material, pasted or glued within a given area. The box lid or frame helps the child to confine his work area. Within it he can arrange and paste the materials. The area to be covered should be small. Show the child how to start pasting on one side or corner of the frame, adhering one small fragment to the tray, placing another next to it, and working towards opposite sides until the whole is covered.

Point out to the child that he can design forms, textures, shadings and shapes through contrast of colour and material as he pastes. The object, in this as in all other such activities, is to allow the child to create his own raw materials. Here the importance of sequence is demonstrably important. The child can tear paper into small, irregular shapes and use them to make mosaics before he can cut with scissors. Later he can cut geometric and other shapes out of coloured paper for similar assembly.

Folding and shaping paper
32 Paper folding

Tools and materials: sheets of bond writing or typing paper; or coloured card; burnisher; or letter-opener with a rounded point; or spoon handle

The ability to fold a square of paper neatly, corner to corner and edge to edge, should be second nature by the time a child goes to school. Demonstrate how to line up one paper edge with another, corner to corner, folding the paper in half neatly and running a finger along the fold once edges and corners meet exactly. The crease should then be burnished with the tool. Unfold the paper to show the crease. Refold and halve the paper a second time, quartering it. Unfold it again.

Most paper folding requires a square piece of paper for a start. With writing and other square-cut papers no measurement is required to turn a rectangle into a square. Take one corner of the paper and bend it over without creasing until one of the two short sides lies directly on top of and parallel to one of the long sides. Holding the parallel edges in position, make a sharp crease first with a finger and then with the burnisher. A section of the paper will extend beyond the folded triangle. Bend this up and over the side of the triangle so that this new crease is parallel to the paper edge. Burnish the crease, open this flap, and tear or cut it off carefully along the crease. When the triangle is opened it will form a perfect square.

Suggest that the child makes several such squares. Let him then fold and refold the square and subsequent triangles corner to corner, burnishing each crease, until the bulk of the paper prevents further folding. Unfold and point out the diagonal and triangular patterns of creases.

33 Accordion folds and pleats

Tools and materials: same as 32

Once a child's arm, hand and finger coordination becomes more refined as a result of simple paper folding, he'll be more adept and deliberate in everything he touches and does. He is now ready for pleating.

Start by folding the paper in half – the long way if it is rectangular. Fold one half of this rectangle in half again and again, each crease parallel to the last (see diagram a) until the first strip is about 1·25 cm ($\frac{1}{2}$″) wide. Unfold. Now, using the first two folded strips as a guide, refold the paper, alternately in one direction and then in the other, to make an accordion pleat (see diagram b).

By using paper clips and rubber bands to hold different portions in place, the pleated paper can be formed and pasted into various shapes (see diagram c).

Lightweight coloured papers offer many design possibilities. Foils can also be used by older children who are sufficiently mature and cautious so as not to cut themselves on sharp corners and edges. Once the principle of accordion pleating is

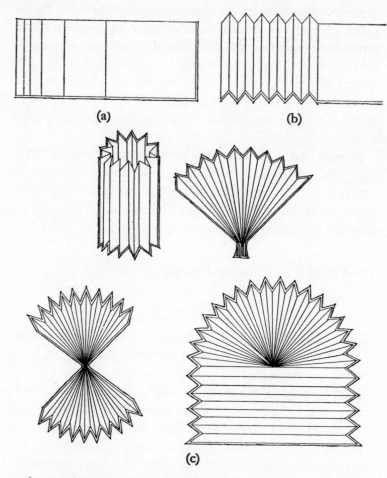

(a)

(b)

(c)

understood, it can be combined with other forms of paper craft and construction (see 39, 40, 42–6, 58–65).

34 Origami for beginners

Tools and materials: square, coloured, lightweight paper (see 32); burnisher (see 32)

No one, regardless of age, can tackle origami with any degree of success until he has perfected the skills described in 32 and

33 above. The following examples are not intended to be copied. Encourage the child to invent his own folds and combinations of folds, and to improvise. He will find delight

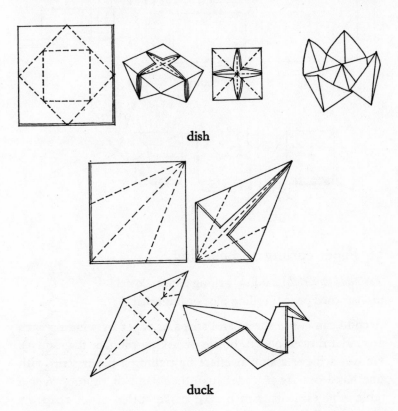

dish

duck

in the shapes he creates. He'll 'see' things, animals and people.

35 Advanced origami

Tools and materials: same as 34

The following are additional and more complex origami folds and constructions that demonstrate some of the possibilities:

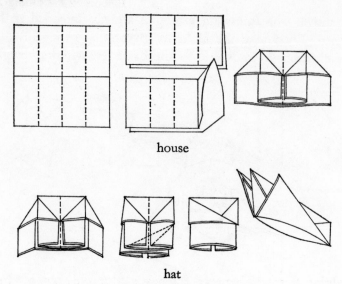

house

hat

36 Paper curling and curving

Tools and materials: card or writing paper; dowel;
unsharpened pencil; rolling pin; or burnisher

A child can curve sheets and strips of paper by winding each
around a dowel, pencil, bottle or rolling pin (see diagram a).
He can achieve a similar effect by pulling a paper strip with
one hand out from under his other hand or thumb, over a
table edge (see diagram b). To make curled paper strips or
shapes, pull the paper over one edge of the burnishing tool,

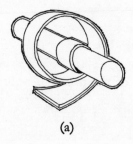

(a)

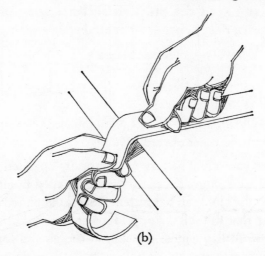

(b)

wedging the strip between the tool's edge and thumb while
pulling.

Embossing and cutting

37 Embossing on paper and foil

Tools and materials: any dull, pointed instrument;
a used-up ballpoint pen; a scriber; or the end of a pointed paint
brush handle; several sheets of blotting paper; masking tape;
writing or any other soft paper; or foil

A pre-schooler can run a scriber across paper or foil taped to
blotting paper. Show him how to make impressions deep
enough to be visible, but sufficiently light so that the paper
does not tear. He can make scribbles, designs, patterns, dots
and dashes. When he turns paper or foil over, he'll discover
his designs raised on the other side. He can deepen the
impressions by scribing along all edges of the raised designs
on the 'wrong' side of the paper. Wooden blocks or letters,
wire or plastic netting, and other raised designs like pastry-
cutters can also be pressed into foil placed on top of several
sheets of blotting paper or a rubber pad. The aim should be

to make embossed designs with a combination of created effects, rather than copying or reproducing existing shapes. (See also 137.)

38 Cutting paper

Tools and materials: school scissors (with rounded points); newspaper; bond paper or card

Don't give your child battery or electrically-operated scissors. Buy good, school-grade scissors with rounded points. Once he matures the child can be trusted with small pointed scissors. Make sure that the scissor grip loops are twisted at an angle so that they fit flat against the skin of thumb and forefinger. Inexpensive scissors do not have twisted grips and they cut into the flesh during extended use. Attach the scissors to your child's worktable or workbench with a long ribbon or string.

The child's cutting will be ragged at first but it will improve in time. He'll acquire greater control faster if he is left without patterns to follow than when these are imposed on him. Encourage pre-schoolers to cut sheets of news- and other paper into snippets at random. Holes can be punched into the cut paper shapes (see 18). They can be laced together (see 20), or used for pasting (see 21–8), collages (see 29) and assemblages (see 30). Later, strips can be cut for paper weaving (see 42–6).

39 Folded-paper cutting

Tools and materials: same as 38

A child can cut along the burnished lines of paper he has learned to fold (see 32–5). Folded and accordion-pleated papers allow the child to make 'interior' cuts in the paper with scissors (see diagram).

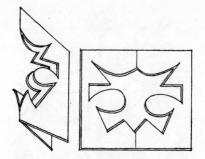

40 Cutting out paper shapes

Tools and materials: scissors; coloured card; drawings and paintings made by the child; photographs and pictures cut from magazines; semi-stiff, starched fabric and felt; ribbons

At this stage of proficiency a child can begin to cut out shapes that interest him from some of the above-listed materials, among others. He can use these cuttings in his collages (see 29) or mount them. Do not show the child how to cut paper flowers, dolls, and other clichés. Let him discover and invent his own forms. Limit what you show the child to basic principles, working method, tool and material use, neat work habits and safety measures appropriate to his or her maturity.

41 Polish paper cuts

Tools and materials: same as 38

Poland has produced its own unique paper folk art. A child can learn to adapt these to his collages and assemblages and to make decorations and paper objects. He will need all or most of the skills described previously in this chapter before he can be expected to manipulate paper in the required manner.

The following diagrams show two of the standard folds and cuts that can be varied, adapted and combined.

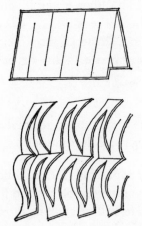

Winding and weaving
42 Paper winding

Tools and materials: rolls of coloured-paper party streamers;
or 1·25cm ($\frac{1}{2}$″) strips of paper pasted together to form long
ribbons; transparent glue (see 26); or paste; or water glass
(sodium silicate), available from chemist's shop

Coil the end of the streamer or ribbon to form a solid core
(see 36). Keep winding, pasting the beginning of the next
strip to the end of the last until a firm and solid round, square
or triangular disc of the desired dimension has been wound
(see diagram a). Paste down the end of the last strip and soak
the whole coil thoroughly in transparent glue, paste or water
glass. Gently press into the centre of the saturated coil to form
a hollow shape (see diagram b), or leave the coil in its original

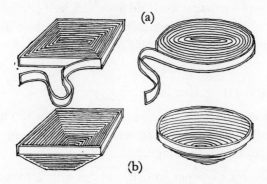

(a)

(b)

state. Such coils can be combined with others to make
mosaics (see 31 and 201), wall hangings and decorations.

43 Paper strips and streamers

Tools and materials: same as 42; small cardboard boxes;
empty, washed glass or plastic bottles

Paper streamers and strips can be wound and pasted around
containers, bins and boxes. Coat one side or part of the

object to be decorated with glue or paste. Wind paper strips or ribbons on to the glued portion. Coat the next section a small area at a time so that it does not dry before it is covered with paper. The child can paste snippets, strips or ribbons of paper side by side, overlapping or criss-crossing one another in any pattern of his or her choice. When the container has been totally covered, paste down all loose paper ends and coat the whole with transparent glue, paste or water glass.

44 Paper weaving

The principles of paper weaving are similar to those required for caning and weaving with fibres, yarn and thread (see Chapter 10). A child can discover the basic processes by first experimenting in paper. They are more understandable when first tried on a loom that the child makes himself (see 45 and 46), weaving with strips that are less flexible than spun fibres and more manageable than reeds.

45 Constructing the loom

Tools and materials: sheets of 21·6cm × 27·9cm (8½″ × 11″) bond paper or coloured card; scissors; sheet of 22·5cm × 30cm (9″ × 12″) cardboard; masking tape

Fold one sheet of paper in half and cut slots into it at right angles to the fold at more or less regular intervals without cutting all the way to the ends of the paper (see diagram). Later,

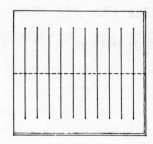

when able to use ruler and triangle, the child can lay out the slots with a pencil, each about 6mm to 12mm ($\frac{1}{4}''$ to $\frac{1}{2}''$) apart. Once the principle is understood, various paper shapes – round, triangular, square, and those used in Polish paper cuts (see 41) or scrolls (cut from adding-machine tape) – can be used to make looms for different paper weaves.

Tape one end of this 'loom' to a sheet of cardboard and it is ready for use.

46 Paper weaves

Tools and materials: paper loom (see 45); coloured card or other papers; scissors; paste (see 21–8)

Cut the paper into strips, each 6mm to 12mm ($\frac{1}{4}''$ to $\frac{1}{2}''$) wide and longer than the loom is wide by at least 2·5cm (1"). Show the child how to start the weave by feeding the first strip over

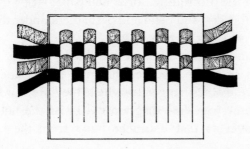

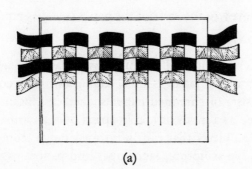

(a)

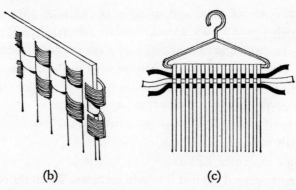

(b)   (c)

and under successive strips of the loom, and the second over and under alternate strips, and so on (see diagram a). Different coloured strips can be used in a variety of ways, or different-coloured strips can be pasted together to achieve different patterns.

When the loom is filled, cut off all but about 6mm ($\frac{1}{4}''$) from each end of the protruding horizontal paper strips that extend beyond both sides, and bend and paste them under the outside vertical strips (see diagram b).

Longer and larger weaves are possible by cutting or pasting long strips of paper together, hanging them, side by side, from a wire clothes-hanger to which they are fastened with tape or clothespegs (see diagram c). Twist the hook of the clothes-hanger so that it can be hung from the back of a chair.

Papier mâché
47 The process

Modelling, building and forming with papier mâché are a favoured craft in Japan, China, India and Mexico. Papier mâché consists of shredded paper soaked in a flour paste or glue, formed as a mash or laid in strips over an armature (see 50–53). The objects that can be formed range from abstract and decorative sculpture, landscapes and panoramas, to play figures, toys, masks, jewellery, pottery and household articles and utensils.

The two basic papier mâché techniques can be used singly or in combination. The mash is useful for forming and moulding small objects, or for sculpting or adding detail to larger constructions. The paper strip technique works best when used in combination with armatures (see 51–3). Other materials – string, twine, tinsel, cloth scraps, ribbon, mesh or netting – can be embedded in or adhered to the papier mâché surface or pressed against it to add textures. When thoroughly dry, papier mâché can be painted (see 56) or waterproofed (see 57).

48 Mash

Tools and materials: newspaper; egg cartons; card and tissue paper, shredded and torn into small pieces; large mixing bowl; flour; water; flour paste (see 24); oil of cloves

Soak the torn and shredded paper for a day and a half in warm water until it turns to pulp. Drain off excess water and squeeze whatever surplus water you can out of the remainder. Mix flour and water to the consistency of double cream. Stir and knead in the pulped paper. The mash should be the consistency of clay for use as a modelling compound. It must be thinned with water until it can be poured if it is to be used as a moulding compound or for adding detail to or decorating papier mâché strip constructions (see 49). Finally, add a few drops of oil of cloves as a preservative.

49 Papier mâché strip construction

Tools and materials: same as 48, except that the paper is torn into strips of different widths

Prepare the same paste mixture detailed in 48. Add a small handful of paper strips to the mixture, letting them soak for ten to fifteen minutes before use. Run each strip through between the second and third finger of one hand to remove excess moisture and paste, before laying it over the armature (see 50–53).

Papier mâché strip construction requires ample working space, arranged so that the child can reach and use all the required materials without confusion (see 10). A wide-based bowl filled with paste is less likely to spill than one that has a narrow base.

50 Armatures

Armatures are essential for working with papier mâché strips and for large modelling and sculpting projects involving mash. An armature is a three-dimensional skeleton of the object to be formed, over which the papier mâché strips (or other modelling compounds) are laid. Armatures can be made out of a large variety of materials (see 51–3).

51 Armatures made out of paper

Tools and materials: newspaper; masking tape; string or twine; scissors

Show the child how to fold, twist, and bundle newspaper into skeleton shapes. Each individual bundle should be taped or tied and then attached to others until the shape of the wanted figure is roughly constructed (see diagram). The armature need only be solid enough so that it can be worked with while the papier mâché strips are laid over it. Once dry, the papier mâché will add strength to the armature and become rigid. When the child is satisfied that the armature approximates the contours of the intended object, show him how to cover it with individual strips of paper soaked in paste (see 49), fleshing out shapes and adding detail with wadded, soaked strips or mash (see 48), adhered with other strips to the main body of the work.

The paste-soaked strips should overlap. Several layers are required until the wall thickness is built up, to withstand usage. When the armature has been covered with one layer,

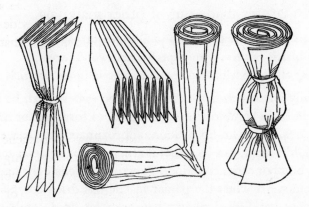

the next should be applied at right angles to the first wherever possible. The width and length of the strips depend on which fit the contours of the object being formed: 5cm × 30cm (2″ × 12″) strips can be used for gently curved or relatively flat surfaces, 2cm × 15cm (¾″ × 6″) strips are required for more acute curves.

52 Armatures made out of cardboard

Tools and materials: light cardboard; shoe or jewellery boxes; corrugated cardboard and boxes; coping saw, jigsaw or keyhole saw (see 92 and 97); sharp mounting or craft knife for more experienced young people (see 69); masking tape

The age, maturity, experience and strength of the child determine which materials and tools he can use. Light cardboard can be cut with large scissors, but heavier cardboard and corrugated cardboard must be cut with a coping saw, keyhole saw or sharp knife. Young children can bend, twist and tape cardboard into desired shapes and, in combination with bundles of newspaper (see 51) and scraps of wood, form armatures. Suggest that, wherever possible, existing shapes are used and combined with others.

53 Armatures made out of other materials

Tools and materials: balloons; sand-filled plastic bags; empty plastic bottles; wire; pipecleaners; wood scraps; pebbles; clay; modelling compounds, among other materials

Virtually any expendable, easily worked material can be used by itself or in combination with others to form papier mâché armatures. A blown-up balloon, approximately the same size as a child's head, can be a useful armature for a papier mâché mask, bowl or other container. Puncture or deflate the balloon and remove it when the papier mâché has dried completely. Paper- or sand-filled plastic bags can be used similarly as armatures for different shapes that need to be hollow when completed. Coat any material that must be separated from the dried papier mâché with a thin layer of Vaseline or vegetable oil before covering it, or the papier mâché may adhere to it.

Pipecleaners (see 114), plastic-covered wire (see 116 and 117), and coat-hanger wire (see 120–22) are useful for armatures that will be totally enclosed with papier mâché. Wire or plastic mesh or netting fastened to the wire armature will cut down on weight and the amount of papier mâché required to cover these armatures.

Wood scraps can be taped or nailed together (see 85–9) and combined with other materials to make larger and more substantial armatures when required.

54 Adding detail to sculptures and objects

Tools and materials: twigs; dowels; paperclips; string; twine; buttons; ribbon; discarded ping-pong, tennis, and other balls; whole and cut-apart egg boxes; bottle tops; and other scrap or discarded parts and materials

Any of these can be embedded in or covered with papier mâché, and added and adhered to armatures or partially completed papier mâché constructions to add detail and texture. Make the child conscious of the possibility of such improvisation whenever possible.

55 Moulding with papier mâché

Moulding is a process with which the child should be familiar. The moulds should consist of household items or they can be improvised or made by the child. A child may wish to duplicate his own work or make multiples – like wheels for a toy he builds.

Show the child how to make the original object. In the case of a wheel, for instance, he will only need to press a dowel end or some other circular object into modelling compound, clay or plaster of Paris (see 197–8). When the mould has dried thoroughly, it must be coated with Vaseline or vegetable oil. Papier mâché mash or strips (see 48 and 49) can then be laid into the open mould. Remove the moulded object after it has dried completely, coat the mould with more Vaseline, and repeat the process for additional identical castings.

Papier mâché shrinks considerably as it dries. Hence there is likely to be some variation between successively cast papier mâché shapes. Do not apply heat or place papier mâché into an oven. It is inflammable, and the slower it dries, the less shrinkage and distortion there will be.

Plastic ice-cube trays and other existing shapes and cavities can be used to mould components for child-originated constructions. They differ from commercially produced toy moulds in so far as they make a demand on the child to discover them, their possibilities, and the uses to which they can be put as a part of his own creations.

56 Painting papier mâché
(See below for required materials.)

When thoroughly dry, papier mâché modelled, sculpted or moulded objects can be painted with any medium. Poster paints (see 149) and acrylics (see 167) are recommended. More mature children who can be relied on to wash hands and brushes with the required solvents and with soap and water after they have completed their work, can use oil paints, japan colours, lacquers and enamels applied in thin, successive layers (see 165–170). Water glass (see 42) or wood sealer (see 107), which closes the pores of the material, is a useful undercoating for these finishes. Or several coats of white poster paint when overpainted with other poster colours or acrylics will bring out their brilliance.

57 Preserving papier mâché objects

Several thin coats of shellac, clear varnish (see 109), water glass (see 42) or transparent glue (see 26), brushed on lightly over fully dry, unpainted or painted papier mâché objects, will strengthen, protect, waterproof and preserve them indefinitely. Wait until each coat is completely dry before applying the next. Never allow a child to use spray cans and, preferably, do not use them yourself (see 11 and 165).

Paper construction
58 Building with paper

Paper construction as a craft for children became popular in Europe around the end of the eighteenth century. At about that time large sheets of paper imprinted with cut-out designs appeared in France, Germany, Holland and England. They included toy houses; dress-up dolls; toy soldiers; theatres and puppets; and panoramas of towns, farms, castles and battle-fields, some printed in black and white, other hand- or stencil-coloured.

Many of these same cut-outs were still available in France twenty years ago, by which time they included three-dimensional railway train, ship, early dirigible, balloon and aeroplane models, similar to those now only available in plastics. The original woodblocks, the stencils by which these early cut-outs were coloured, and the paper construc-tions of the past can now be seen only in museums. More recent published paper constructions include a working model of a pendulum clock, every gear and part made out of paper, that can still be bought in France today.

During the past seventy-five years paper and cardboard construction became a craft employed by architects, engineers, artists and designers. As a craft medium for children it requires experience in some of the more fundamental skills detailed in earlier portions of this chapter.

59 Slot construction

Tools and materials: a deck of old playing cards;
or rectangular file cards; or cardboard or heavy card;
scissors

Demonstrate how cuts can be made into the sides of cards so that each can be slotted to the next, slot to slot (see diagram a). Cards with cuts made at right angles to their sides up to and slightly beyond the centre can be slotted together so that they will stand on a more or less level surface. Four square or rectangular cards with two such slots cut into one side each will form a free-standing box that needs only top and bottom pasted or taped to it to enclose it fully. Show the child the dividers in corrugated food and beverage cartons that are joined in just such a manner. A child can use this principle for a great variety of paper and cardboard construction. Paper plates and cups and lightweight cardboard tubes can be jointed in the same way (see diagram b and diagrams a and b on page 73).

To stimulate the use of this principle in children's paper and cardboard craft, I originated a toy, The Builder, first shown in New York's Museum of Modern Art in 1953. That year Charles Eames, the furniture designer, created his House of Cards, coincidentally employing the same principle although in a slightly varied form. Both toys, enjoyed by several generations of children, have since been copied widely. Regrettably, such playthings are given to children as substitutes rather than as inspirations for craft activities.

When slotting material thicker than card, and especially when using cardboard (see 67), the slots should be cut a

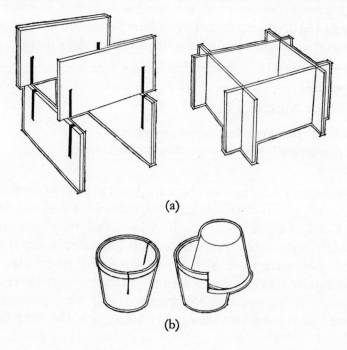

(a)

(b)

shade wider than the thickness of the material or else it will buckle and fray at the joints when pieces are slotted together.

60 Paper joints and levers

Tools and materials: light cardboard; old playing cards; file cards; scissors; hole punch (see 18); paperclips; or grommet set (see 19) and hammer; string or twine; heavy sheet of cardboard, plywood, or scrap wood for working surface

Jointed paper dolls and jumping jacks were among the first European paper toys produced during the late seventeen hundreds. They were children's favourites, then as now. In Europe, jointed paper dolls were printed on lightweight paper and sold as penny sheets. They needed to be mounted on stiffer paper or cardboard, cut out, and assembled with string. Any child can use these principles of paper jointing to create a great variety of playthings, mobile constructions and lever-operated toys.

Cut the paper or card stock into strips 2·5cm × 12·7cm (1″ × 5″) or longer, punch a hole at both ends of each (see 18), insert grommets, and join one to the next with string or paperclips (see diagram a). The same principle, using paper

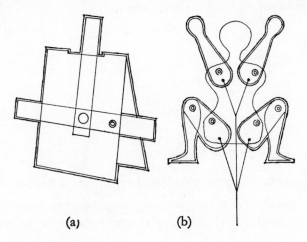

(a)   (b)

strips as levers, can be employed to make mobile and animated toys, mechanisms, and designs (see diagram b).

61 Scoring paper with a scriber

Tools and materials: soft pencil; ruler; card; scriber;
used-up ballpoint pen, or other dull, pointed instrument

Paper construction often requires sharp folds (see 32–5 and 41) and creases. Sometimes the texture and weight of the paper cause ordinary folds to be uneven or wavy, or to crack. Heavy or textured papers should always be crease-scored with a scriber before they are folded.

Draw a line with pencil and ruler from one side of the paper to the other, or wherever the paper is to be folded. Then place the ruler so that the line is just visible. Next, run the scriber along the ruler's edge, pressing on the point sufficiently hard to emboss the paper without breaking its surface. It will then fold easily along the scored line.

Wavy, round and semi-circular scores can be made free-hand or along templates (see 65). Such scores are especially effective in paper sculpture (see 73). When combined with straight scores and cuts, curved scores lend dimension and texture to paper design (see diagram).

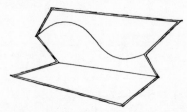

62 Scoring with a knife

Tools and materials: same as 61; metal-edge ruler; Stanley knife

Heavy paper and cardboard require cut-scores before they can be folded. Obviously this is not to be done by young children. Instead of using the scriber (see 61), run the knife blade along the marked line and the metal edge of the ruler, cutting no deeper than halfway through the material. It will then bend without cracking. Needless to say, the material is substantially weakened at such a fold and may require tape or other interior support in some constructions. (Observe the safety cautions suggested in 69 when making such cuts.)

63 Planning and layout

At early stages all paper construction should be spontaneous and improvised. When the design has reached its ultimate pleasing shape, it may be a mass of small pieces joined to one another. Component forms can then be disassembled, laid out flat, and used as templates. Reconstruction from these templates requires some use of draughting instruments in many cases. Even before he can count, add and subtract, a child can learn to use a compass, triangles and a ruler for simple geometric designing.

The following describes some of the designing skills that are useful in paper construction. Be sure to encourage the child to develop a form spontaneously as a paper mock-up (see 64) before he details his design and works it out more precisely. Placement of folds, scores, glue laps and tabs must first be established by trial and error and by improvisation before they can be placed with precision.

64 Paper mock-ups

Tools and materials: card or heavy bond paper; scissors;
scriber (see 61) or scoring board; masking tape, paperclips,
stapler and paste

There are many ways of constructing an ordinary paper cube or box. Teaching a child one or all of the various methods is futile. He must experiment spontaneously before he can understand construction principles. Let him cut out pieces of paper and join them with tape, paperclips or a stapler to form solid shapes. They may not be neat and square, but he'll discover methods of construction – what works and what doesn't.

This technique is useful for discovering and inventing geometric as well as non-geometric organic forms. In working in this manner, it soon becomes obvious that different weights of paper and other supplementary materials can be useful or are essential in various portions of a complex structure.

A young child will be perfectly satisfied with such a relatively crude mock-up. Rough construction details can be covered with coloured paper or poster paints. At later stages young people may wish to execute more-finished versions after working out construction details on their paper mock-ups.

65 Paper templates

A paper or any other template is simply a shape worked out so that it can be reproduced or traced on to another piece of material. For example, it is easier to design a single equilateral triangle and, having made a template of it, to repeat it as often as necessary, than to construct a whole figure geometrically throughout.

The paper mock-up (see 64), cut apart and unfolded, can become a rough model for a more-finished and precise template made with ruler, compass, triangle and other draughting instruments. A final template can then be constructed to be copied, reproduced or repeated as many times as required.

66 Glue laps

Tools and materials: same as 64 and 65

The mock-up may contain one or more sides that need to be fastened to other edges. One method of making such joints neatly requires the addition of a glue lap to one of each set of two sides that are to be fastened (see diagram a). Each such glue lap should be slightly shorter than the length of the side to which it is to be attached so that the corners don't bulk and buckle when the two matching edges are pasted together.

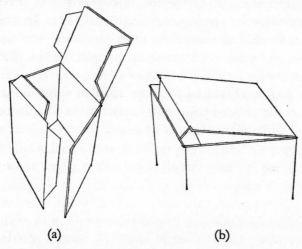

(a)   (b)

Each glue lap should be pasted to the underside of the paper edge to which it is to be attached.

When making geometric constructions like a cube or a box, the side to which a glue lap is attached should be shorter by the thickness of the material used than the other sides (see diagram b). Add each required glue lap to the template or layout, score the line where glue lap and side are joined, bend the glue lap down, and paste it to the underside of the matching edge.

Cardboard construction
67 Building with cardboard

Collages, assemblages, designs, models, toys, usable child- and adult-size furniture and storage spaces can be made entirely out of cardboard or corrugated cardboard or with these materials in combination with others. Cardboard 'carpentry' has become something of a separate craft. It is a useful preparation for working in wood. Most of the methods employed can be used for both wood and paper.

Cardboard is a mixture of raw wood pulp, scrap paper and cloth fibres, cooked and pressed, like paper (see 13), into un-bleached sheets of varying thickness. First used as a packaging material in the nineteenth century, cardboard has become increasingly important as construction material as well.

Cardboard is available in a large variety of grades, ranging from soft, pulpy board used for egg cartons, to heavier boards lined on one or both sides with paper. The latter are used for folding and set-up boxes and posters. Still better grades include poster board, illustration board, backing boards for pads of drawing and writing paper, and binder's board used for library bindings of books. Fluted, corrugated cardboard is now available in several plies also. In addition, there exists a range of composition boards consisting of paper or cardboard laminated to thin sheets of plywood, foam-core plastics and asbestos, used mostly for packaging and building insulation. Finally, there are cardboard tubes that are available in a range of wall thicknesses, diameters, lengths and strengths. All of them, with the exception of asbestos board, make excellent craft materials for young people. Asbestos board tends to crumble, and the dust, if inhaled, is a health hazard.

Raw or lined cardboard and corrugated board can be used as it is or painted (see 149 and 165–9). Raw cardboard can be primed before painting with other than poster paints (see 107). It can also be lined with white or coloured paper or foil (see 22–8 and 68).

68 Laminating paper and foil to cardboard

Tools and materials: cardboard or corrugated board;
white or coloured papers and foils; paste or glue (see 22–8)

It is easier and quicker to laminate large sheets of paper to
cardboard before cutting it up into small pieces. When covering
large areas of paper and cardboard with paste, use a square of
cardboard as a spreader instead of a brush.

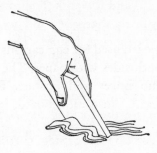

69 Using sharp tools and knives
(See also 11 and 82.)

Until he is sufficiently experienced and reliable, even an older
child should not work with sharp tools except under close
adult supervision. Anyone is bound to cut himself at some
time while using them. The relative severity or harmlessness
of such cuts depends on observance of simple but imperative
safety rules. To deprive children of developing the necessary

self-discipline and caution means to invite possibly serious
injury later. My five-year-old daughter and four-year-old son,
practised in craft since earliest ages, have learned to cut
linoleum blocks with sharp gouges, under supervision,
without harming themselves.

Set the stage for eventual careful use of potentially dangerous tools by introducing children to simple and safe ones at early ages and by insisting on the same precautions and disciplines in their use as for those they will need later. The following precautions are worth observing:

a. Never walk about holding a pair of scissors or a knife, unless absolutely necessary. Then carry the tool by the handle, blade pointing ahead and towards the ground.

b. Provide only finely sharpened and honed, rust-free tools inserted into an appropriate holder. The handle should be long enough to fit the child's hand, allowing him to hold the tool without touching the blade itself. Dull, ragged or rusty tools cause serious and infected injuries.

c. Check before use the locking device that holds a knife blade in its holder and assure that there is no 'play' in the blade.

d. When not in use store the tool, metal parts lightly coated with oil or Vaseline, wrapped in wax paper, in a cloth or leather sheath or in a tool rack, out of reach of young children.

e. To cut paper foil or cardboard with a knife blade: Draw the line along which the cut is to be made with a pencil and a ruler or T-square. Cut only along the edge of a metal T-square (see diagram); never use a straight-edge (it can slip), or a plastic or wooden edge, along which to run a knife. Hold

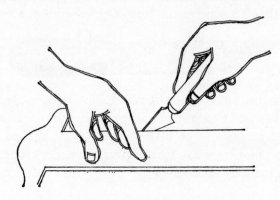

the knife in one hand and the T-square down on to the paper or board with the fingers of the other hand spread apart. Check the position of the fingers on the T-square before cutting, to make sure that no fingertip projects beyond the metal edge along which the cut is to be made. Make several passes with the knife blade along the pencil line using the metal edge as the guide. Never attempt to cut through heavy paper or even lightweight cardboard with a single pass of the blade.

f. Teach young people to keep their eyes on the blade while cutting: never to look away, even for a moment, and to stop cutting if their attention is required elsewhere.

g. Demonstrate how to keep the hand holding the T-square or the material *behind* the knife blade and never ahead of it. This is especially important when whittling or carving wood, cutting wood and linoleum blocks, and using chisels and gouges. Always make cuts or gouge material in a direction away from the hand holding the material.

h. Sharp knives and tools momentarily laid aside on the worktable should be embedded in a kneaded eraser.

i. Teach young people how to hold sharp and pointed tools.

j. Keep a first-aid kit near work areas. The kit should include Band-Aids, bandage, surgical tape, mild disinfectant, a rubber band to use as a temporary tourniquet, and a tube of Vaseline.

70 Flexible, fluted cardboard strips

Flexible, fluted cardboard, more malleable than the corrugated kind, can be bought in rolls or found, used as protective wadding and as buffers in containers for large appliances. It can be cut into strips with scissors or a knife, bent parallel with the fluting (cut-scored for folds at right angles to the fluting), rolled, curved and coiled, glued, taped or stapled to itself and to other materials. It is especially useful for making armatures (see 50–53 and 195) and as a base for papier mâché, clay, or plaster panoramas or landscapes.

71 Corrugated cardboard

Cut-apart grocery cartons or sheets of corrugated board can be cut into various shapes with a sharp knife blade or with a coping saw, keyhole saw or back saw. It can be bent parallel to the fluting without scoring. Bends at right angles to the fluting require cut scores (see 62). Several layers of corrugated board, laminated to each other, are sufficiently strong for large collages, assemblages and life-size, usable tables, chairs, storage shelves and other furniture, as well as play material, building blocks and toy vehicles on which the child can ride, and life-size dolls' houses and play shops.

Slot construction (see 59) provides greatest strength and flexibility. Tape the edges of finished corrugated board constructions with packaging tape to prevent fraying and separation of the cover papers from the fluting. Corrugated cardboard can be painted like any other paper or cardboard (see 67).

72 Cardboard tubes

Cardboard tubes, cut into different lengths with a sharp knife blade, coping saw, keyhole saw or back saw, are useful in three-dimensional design, in assemblages, or as components like table and chair legs in combination with other materials. They can be pasted, tied, taped or jointed.

Semi-circular cross-laps can be cut into the ends of cardboard tubes with a saw. Use one such cut-off as a template for marking identical joints into other tube ends. Several tubes, notched in this manner, will fit together like logs used to build a cabin (see diagram b). Slot jointed tube ends can fit to slot jointed flat cardboard shapes (see diagram a).

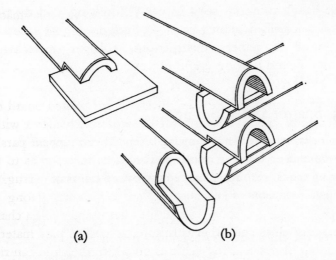

(a)   (b)

Paper sculpture
73 Formed paper relief

Tools and materials: white and coloured card; fluted cardboard;
scissors; sharp knife blade (see 62 and 69); scriber;
scoring board; Cellophane tape; masking tape; stapler;
paste (see 22–8); heavy cardboard base

Paper can be sculpted in relief by cutting, scoring and folding
(see 32–6, 41–3 and 58–66). Such sculpture should not be
attempted until the different methods of paper folding, cutting
and scoring have been explored.

For spontaneous paper sculpture a wood or heavy cardboard base is essential. Paper shapes can be curved and curled
and attached to it with tape, paste or staples. These shapes can
be given three-dimensional detail and texture (see 61).

Making decorative papers
74 Techniques and methods

Paper making is beyond the scope of this book (see 13). But a
child can create interesting and decorative papers by pasting

(see 21–9), printing (see Chapter 8), drawing, and the techniques described below (see 75–6). Such decorative papers can be used in paper constructions, collages, assemblages, sculpting and making useful objects.

75 Spatter and stippling

Tools and materials: white drawing or bond paper; sponge; toothbrush or stippling brush; bowl of clean water; poster paints (see 149); clean, empty baby food jars; tongue depressors or lolly sticks

Prepare thick poster paint mixtures, each colour in its own jar. Show the child how to dip sponge or brush into the paint and then dab it lightly on to the paper. The lighter the touch, the more interesting and varied the effects will be. After stippling one sheet with a single colour, wash out the sponge or brush, squeeze it dry, and use a second colour, as before. A third colour and more can be added in turn, either while previous coatings are still wet or after they have dried. A great many different effects and colour mixtures can be achieved in this way. (See also 156 for another spatter effect.)

76 Ink-patterned paper

Tools and materials: white drawing or bond paper; India ink in various colours; eyedropper, one for each colour; sponge; bowl of clear water; sheets of newspaper or blotting paper; coloured felt markers (optional)

Place the drawing paper on top of several layers of newspaper or on to heavy blotting paper. Moisten the drawing paper with water and sponge. Drop blots of coloured ink on to the moistened paper, using the eyedropper. The inks will crawl and bleed, creating a variety of patterns and designs. Several different colours can be used in succession. Additional variation can be achieved by dropping small amounts of soapy water into the design, again using an eyedropper. Do not disturb or move the paper until the water and inks have dried thoroughly.

Such moistened paper can also be flooded with watercolour applied with a brush, which is then drawn into with coloured felt marker and drawing pens dipped into India ink. These and other 'resist' methods (see 159 and 166) can be combined with each other.

3 Carpentry

Life without industry is guilt, industry without art is brutality.
John Ruskin

77 Background

Carpentry invokes the smell, feel and texture of wood and wood shavings and of hand-held tools. Wood is a vanishing resource. Today's farming, printing, building, packaging, plastics and chemical industries eat into the surviving and replanted reservoir of forests at a rate faster than they can regenerate. But trees are not only a source of prime raw materials. They are the major converters of carbon dioxide into breathable oxygen. For all these reasons wood will certainly become a treasured commodity once again, used discreetly as a craft material. This will also stimulate a revival of interest in its unique properties, care in its use, and preservation.

As a first introduction to carpentry, cardboard – corrugated

and chip – and the various wall and composition boards are as useful as wood and sometimes more so. They are softer and easier to saw, joint and work and they are usually less expensive. Therefore many of the projects described in this chapter apply equally to materials other than wood on which carpentry tools can be used (see 58–72).

78 Carpentry tools

Today's production and hobby carpentry involves the use of a profusion of power tools. But the judgement demanded for working in wood requires training in and use of simple hand tools, not only as a learning process for young people but also as preparation for an eventual use of machinery. Sawing, hammering, drilling, jointing and other operations in woodworking require a familiarity with the characteristics of the raw material that can only be gained from working with hand tools.

There's a knack to driving a nail with a hammer that, if it becomes second nature, frees a child or young person so that he can concentrate on the creative aspects of crafts. There are efficient ways of using a screwdriver, a hand drill or a saw, setting up work, preparing jigs or making a mortise, so that the process of creation can take precedence over production (see 5). These operations require experience that, cumulatively, lays the foundation on which more advanced skills can be built.

But it's not enough to give a child a hand-tool kit or a workbench. He needs experiences and an outlook that make it possible for him to use carpentry tools imaginatively and with a purpose. He needs to be given raw materials on which to exercise tools, skills and his own ideas. He needs guidance to enable him to understand that the purpose of the exercise of his skills is expression and not mere production.

It is important to give a child only one or two tools at a time, together with materials on which they can be used. They should be presented so that he is encouraged to explore them and be inventive. He also needs to be shown basic craft disciplines and have some of the possible effects of violating them explained to him.

Some parents and teachers are afraid to give carpentry tools to young children. They worry that a child might hurt himself, misuse the tools, or create havoc among siblings or furniture. Yet children to whom materials are properly introduced, who are fired with enthusiasm for creating self-originated ideas and objects, and who are given guidance, are not likely to misuse tools. As pointed out earlier, anything is

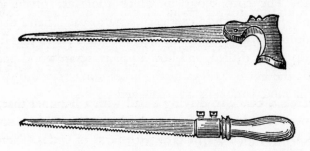

dangerous in the hands of an undisciplined or inexperienced child.

Tools for children are best bought from educational, jeweller's, art supply and hardware shops, rather than in toy shops. Most professional tools come in a variety of sizes and weights, some sufficiently small and light that they fit the hands of children mature enough to use them. An upholsterer's tack hammer, of which the handle has been shortened, makes an excellent child's carpentry hammer. Model makers' and jewellers' coping saws fit the hands of any five-year-old. A regular compass, keyhole, wallboard, dovetail saw or back saw is far more useful and workable than the miniature cross-cut saws usually found in children's toy tool chests. And they are much less dangerous. The least expensive, lightweight carpenter's hand drill is preferable to its shoddy toy counterpart and is no more expensive.

79 When to provide tools

Give the child a new tool only when he can hold it properly. If the smallest or lightest-weight professional tool is too heavy or difficult to hold and guide, then the child should not be expected to work with it. The same principle applies to the material. A child mature enough to handle a coping saw may not have the strength and endurance to saw through 3mm ($\frac{1}{8}$") plywood. Give him balsa, wallboard or soft cardboard instead. The chronology in which tools are given is important. Before a child can learn how to use a hand drill, he must know how to clamp the wood to the table so that it does not slip when drilled, and how to place scrap wood under it so that the bottom edges of the holes don't fray and splinter and the table surface is not damaged.

80 Spontaneity and planning

The more advanced forms of carpentry, like all other craft, require planning, measurement, marking, and transfer of designs for parts that are to be sawed, drilled or jointed. But don't teach a child how to mark or saw along a straight line, or how to joint or make objects that require numerical or geometric measurement, until he has experienced spontaneous craft. The meaning and purpose of numbers, measures, weights and proportions can become clear only when the child has the maturity, skills and desire to apply them to creative ends.

81 Work spaces

Carpentry involves work that can ruin household or school furniture. Most commercially made children's worktables and benches (other than those made for school use) are inadequate, expensive and last for only a short time. As an alternative to the trestle worktable (see 10) that is adjustable as the child grows, a tabletop workbench can be made in any home or school workshop. It can be stored when not in use.

82 Safety

Carpentry requires some special precautions, which are detailed for each tool and project to which they apply. (See also 11 and 69.) Teach the child to be especially conscious of the hand and fingers that hold the material while wood is sawed, drilled, gouged or chiselled, or a nail driven. Insist that a vice or clamp holds the material to the table whenever possible, instead of holding in the hand. Whenever the child uses sharp tools, chisels, knives, gouges or even a screwdriver, the hand resting on or holding the material should always be well away from, behind, and out of the way of the stroke of the tool.

First projects
83 Preparation for play

Tools and materials: large wooden building blocks;
peg and hole toys; wooden or plastic nuts, bolts, and slats;
wrench; workbench; wooden mallet and wooden screwdriver

These toys are essential preparation for later craft skills and interests. Piling building blocks on top of one another and fitting pegs to matching holes are not only exercises in co-ordination; they stimulate understanding of which shapes fit and which don't, and of relative sizes. Large plastic or wooden nuts and bolts and sanded wooden slats with holes drilled through them so that they can be bolted together, with a large wooden or small metal wrench to tighten the bolts, and similar toys, prepare the child for insights and skills he will need for carpentry as for other craft and learning.

A workbench is the most useful first tool kit for children one and a half to three years old. Remove all tools but the mallet at the start. Teach the child to hold it near the end of the handle and not near the head, as young children are wont to do. Suggest that he or she keeps eyes fixed on the peg to be hammered and the other hand well out of harm's way.

84 Tack hammering

Tools and materials: splinter-free, well-sanded, short lengths of
5cm × 5cm (2″ × 2″) wood; several boxes of long-stemmed
drawing pins or carpet tacks; tack hammer with shortened
handle; G-clamp (see 90)

At nursery school or kindergarten age a child who has enjoyed preparatory experiences (see 83) should possess sufficient
coordination to use a small hammer to drive tacks into planks.
Show him how to start the tack by holding and tapping it
gently into wood clamped to the worktable. He can hammer
designs with coloured tacks.

85 Nailing

Tools and materials: splinter-free, well-sanded 5cm (2″) thick
wood scraps; lath; tongue depressors; carpet tacks or roofing
nails; tack hammer with shortened handle;
25 × 25 × 2cm (10″ × 10″ × ¾″) plywood as a work surface

Do not give young children small-headed brads or common or
finishing nails to hammer. They are difficult to strike. Roofing
nails have extra-large heads and are therefore especially useful
at early ages.

Set the child up at his or her worktable or workbench (see
10 and 81) or, if the work is to be done at a regular table, make
sure that a wooden workboard is provided. Then show the
child how to nail lath and tongue depressors to scrap wood
shapes. Demonstrate how a single nail only hinges the lath
to the wood; a second and third nail will hold it firmly. Teach
the child to check the length of the nail against the depth of
layers of wood he plans to join before nailing them together
so that the nail ends do not protrude beyond the material
(see diagram a).

You may have to show the child repeatedly how the nail
must be started at a slight angle away from the carpenter, and

held between fingers only until the point has penetrated the wood and the nail can stand up by itself; and how the hammer should be held (see diagram b). Point out that the hammer's head will strike the nail squarely if he keeps his eyes fixed on

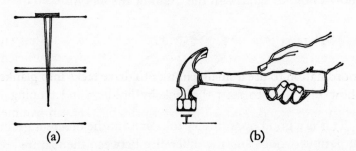

(a)   (b)

the nail's head. Teach him how to tap the nail rather than hit it hard. Then let him work on his own and discover the different ways of nailing pieces of wood to each other.

86 The nail set

Tools and materials: same as 85; common nails; nail set

Once the child is adept at nailing with large-headed roofing nails and tacks, he can be given common nails of various lengths. A nail set can now be added to his tool kit. It will enable him to drive common nailheads slightly below the surface of the wood for a better and safer finish.

87 Sandpapering

Tools and materials: bag of wood scraps and cut-offs, obtainable from timber yard or woodworking shop;
two blocks of wood, each 5 cm × 7·5 cm × 2·5 cm (2″ × 3″ × 1″)
(more or less); two sheets of medium sandpaper;
two sheets of fine sandpaper

Cut the sheets of sandpaper with scissors so that they fit round the wooden blocks. Tape or staple one sheet of each grade of sandpaper to the blocks, sandpaper side facing out (see diagram). Then let the child sand scrap wood until it is splinter-free and smooth, using the coarser paper first and then the finer one to obtain a good finish. The child must be shown how to sand with the grain of the wood.

This is a good opportunity to point out the different grains of various woods and the difference between the texture and appearance of end grain and that running lengthwise on the board. Show the child how the wood is marred when sanded against the grain.

88 Gluing
(See 21–8 for tools and materials.)

For use by children and young people, most of the recommended pastes and adhesives serve wood as well as paper, with only a few exceptions. Wallpaper and flour pastes and cow gum do not bond wood effectively.

Commercially available casein glues, mucilage and acrylics are recommended for children's carpentry projects. Show the child how to apply a minimum of adhesive and yet cover one or both surfaces with an even coating of glue. Have him wipe away excess glue around joints with a damp cloth before the glue begins to set. Later he can use clamps to hold pieces of wood together while the glue dries (see 90). The child must learn to be patient and not to disturb glued joints and surfaces until the adhesive has set completely.

89 Collages and assemblages

Tools and materials: sanded scrap wood (see 87); lath;
tongue depressors; scrap and waste wood turnings and moulding;
tack hammer (see 85); assortment of common nails, each size
kept in its own screw-top glass jar or in separate compartments
of an egg carton; paste (see 21–8);
30cm × 30cm × 2cm (12″ × 12″ × ¾″) pine or plywood board, to
be used as a base or working surface

The child can nail different shapes of wood on top of and next
to one another on to the board, or make an open or partially
enclosed hollow framework (see diagram), or combine both
techniques. When completed, they can be painted (see 106–10
and Chapter 6). (See also 29 and 30.)

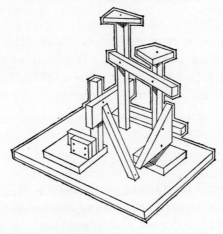

Carpentry for beginners
90 Clamping

Tools and materials: two G-clamps; two corner clamps;
two model maker's or wood hand-screw clamps

Once a child enjoys woodworking, clamping will expedite
gluing and other operations. He can then attempt more
ambitious projects.

It doesn't matter if the wood is marred or scratched during a child's early carpentry efforts. Nevertheless it is important to instil care and good work habits as early as possible. Teach the child to keep a scrap of wood or lath between the jaws of any metal clamp he may use and the outside surfaces of the wood that is held. When the wood is protected in this manner, G-clamps can be useful for nailing and gluing. Corner clamps enable the child to join wooden pieces at perfect right angles (see 97). The model maker's and wood hand-screw clamps are designed for more delicate work.

91 The vice

Tools and materials: carpenter's vice

Once a child understands the purpose of clamps, he'll benefit from being given a carpenter's vice. It is available at any hardware shop and can be attached to a trestle table (see 10), table-top workbench (see 81) or any other worktable. A combination of clamps and vice is the equivalent of several extra pairs of hands.

92 The coping saw or jigsaw

Tools and materials: jeweller's or other coping saw;
coping saw workbench attachment (see diagram b)
package of spiral coping saw blades; box lids;
or 10cm × 15cm × 3mm (4″ × 6″ × $\frac{1}{8}$″) cardboard;
gummed white paper sheets, each about 6mm ($\frac{1}{4}$″) larger all around than the cardboard or balsa (if no pre-gummed paper is available, white drawing paper or bond paper and paste will serve the same ends); box of wax crayons; scissors;
15cm × 22cm (6″ × 9″) manilla envelopes

The diagram shows how the coping saw workbench attachment can be made if none is available in local hardware or craft shops. Without it a child will find it difficult to use a coping saw effectively.

Let the child draw a picture or design on to the paper. Make

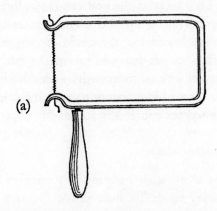

(a)

sure that the whole paper surface is covered with colour. Paste the drawing to the cardboard and trim off any excess paper. Clamp the workbench attachment to the table. Insert

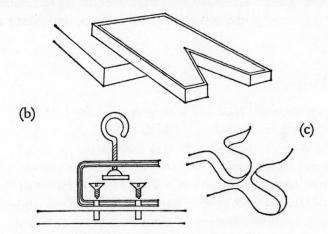

(b)

(c)

a spiral saw blade into the jaws of the coping saw. A child cannot cut himself with such a blade while working with it. Show him how to hold the saw by the handle after he is seated before the table. Saw cuts should be made inside the V-shaped

notch of the workbench attachment. Then suggest that the
child cuts the picture into as many small pieces as he chooses.
He'll make his own jigsaw puzzle.

Demonstrate how to start the first cut (and all future cuts)
by moving the saw blade up and down gently against the
edge of the material, keeping the blade as perpendicular as
possible. Any five- or six-year-old can make such a puzzle
without difficulty at one or more work sessions. He can put
the cut-apart pieces of his puzzle into an envelope as a gift.
Once he becomes proficient in the use of the coping saw, he
can be shown how to cut interlocking puzzle pieces (see
diagram c) and other shapes.

Note: For other work with a coping saw involving interior
cuts, it is necessary to drill a hole inside the area to be cut
away (see 93), large enough so that the coping saw blade can
be inserted through it before it is fitted to the saw itself. Then
attach the blade to the saw handle and cut away the interior
portion. If any blade other than a spiral blade is used, be sure
that the teeth of the blade face *down* when inserted into the
coping saw.

93 Drilling

Tools and materials: hand drill with 6mm ($\frac{1}{4}''$) chuck;
assorted drill bits, including 6mm ($\frac{1}{4}''$) bit;
coping saw (see 92); mallet; 6mm ($\frac{1}{4}''$) dowel;
sandpaper (see 87); carpenter's vice or G-clamps (see 90 and 91);
sheets of 15cm × 15cm × 2cm (6″ × 6″ × $\frac{3}{4}''$) pine or plywood (to
be drilled); one sheet of 20cm × 20cm × 2cm (8″ × 8″ × $\frac{3}{4}''$) pine
or plywood (to be placed under the wood to be drilled);
set square (see 99); pencil

Let the child sand the wood to be drilled until it is splinter-
free and smooth. Then show him how to clamp it into the vice
for horizontal drilling of the surface (see diagram a) or ver-

tical drilling of the edge (see diagram b), or flat to the table with G-clamps for vertical drilling. Place the larger piece of scrap wood behind or underneath the wood to be drilled. It will assure a clean hole and it protects the table or other surface from being penetrated by the drill bit. Insert the 6mm ($\frac{1}{4}$") bit into the chuck of the drill and tighten it firmly. Then

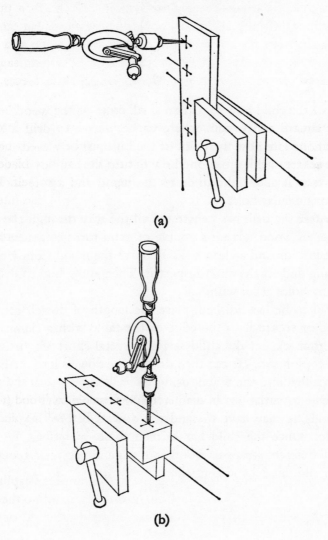

(a)

(b)

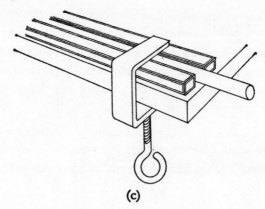

(c)

show the child how to mark a small cross on the wood, using set square and pencil, wherever he wishes to drill a hole. Demonstrate how the point of the bit must be placed against the centre of this cross, and how to turn the handle of the drill to keep it at a right angle to the wood and assure a clean, perpendicular hole.

After the drill has penetrated all the way through the first layer of wood, give it a couple of extra turns to assure total penetration and a clean hole. Remove the wood from vice or clamp and let the child inspect it. Then allow him to drill as many holes as he wishes.

When he has finished, place the length of dowel into the vice or secure it to the edge of the table with a clamp (see diagram c). Let the child saw off several short lengths with his coping saw. He can then drive these dowels into the holes he drilled into the wood, using his mallet.

Due to variations in diameter and possible swelling of the wood, he may have to sand the dowels before they fit the holes. Once the child has learned these operations, he can drill different scraps of wood and lath and peg them together to build, model and construct.

94 The wrench

Tools and materials: same as 93; nuts and 6mm ($\frac{1}{4}''$) bolts in different lengths; small adjustable wrench

Once the child has learned to drill holes into the wood and lath, he can join them with nuts and bolts. Strips of lath, drilled and bolted to others and to pieces of scrap wood, will familiarize him with levers. Empty cotton reels bolted to drilled wood enable him to invent moving designs, mechanisms and toys.

95 The screwdriver

Tools and materials: small screwdriver; small flat-headed screws; hand drill and bits (see 93); 2cm ($\frac{3}{4}''$) soft pine scrap wood; lath; tongue depressors; 20cm × 20cm × 2cm ($8'' \times 8'' \times \frac{3}{4}''$) pine board or plywood (to be placed under the wood as it is drilled and screwed together)

There is no point in giving a child a screwdriver until he has learned how to use a drill. Unless holes are pre-drilled slightly smaller than the diameter of the shank of the screws, a screwdriver is extremely hazardous and difficult to use. Unlike nails, screws should never be held in the hand while a screwdriver is used; the tool can slip and inflict a deep and painful wound. Insert the pointed end of the screw into the hole and turn it hand-tight before using the screwdriver.

Clamp two pieces of wood, one quarter again as thick, when clamped, as the screws are long, to the table or into the vice, together with the 2cm ($\frac{3}{4}''$)-thick backing board. Select a bit slightly smaller in diameter than the screw to be used. Insert it into the chuck of the drill and drill a hole through the two pieces of wood that are to be joined, no deeper than three-quarters of the way through the second piece. Show the child how to check the screw length against the thickness of the two pieces of wood to assure that the sharp point of the screw will not penetrate the far side after it is screwed into the wood (see diagram). Then screw the two pieces of wood together.

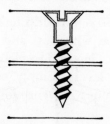

Once the child has observed and understood these various operations, he needs ample opportunity to practise on his own.

96 Countersink

Tools and materials: same as 95; countersink

The top of the shank of any screw is slightly larger than the threaded part. Hence the head is likely to protrude above the surface of the wood unless it is forced into it. Show the child how to insert the countersink into the chuck of the hand drill to enlarge the hole he first drilled into the wood, so that the screw, once fully driven into the wood with the screwdriver, lies flush with the surface of the wood or slightly below it.

97 Mitre box and back saw

Tools and materials: back saw (for younger children provide a keyhole, wallboard or compass saw); mitre box;
set square (see 99); pencil; two G-clamps and two corner clamps (see 90); 5cm × 25cm × 1·25cm (2″ × 10″ × ½″) pine board

Clamp the mitre box to the table edge firmly. Place the pine board inside it (see diagram). Demonstrate the different cuts that can be made by placing the saw into the different slots cut into the mitre box. Show the child how 90° and 45° cut pieces can be joined for gluing, nailing and screwing. Corner clamps are useful for demonstrating some of the possible joints, as well as for holding the cut wood in place for jointing.

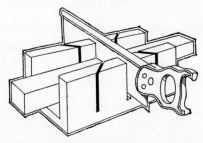

It is important that the child learns how to hold the saw properly from the very start, using the 'pistol grip' with index finger extended as a guide. This assures the most effective control of any hand saw. The mitre box is the best introduction to sawing since it teaches the importance of maintaining the proper angle of the saw to achieve the desired cut. Once the child understands these operations and requirements, he is ready to saw. Later he can learn to mark the lines (see 98–102). He must then line up the marked line with the appropriate mitre box slot.

Starting the cut without fraying the wood is a matter of practice and experience. Start at one edge of the wood with short, quick strokes of the saw blade until the teeth make a small notch within which they remain. Then, using longer, even strokes of the saw, the wood can be cut all the way through. When the child nears the end of his cut, he must shorten the strokes of the saw once more so that the further edges of the board do not splinter at the finish.

If the saw blade frays the wood, either the saw is not held perpendicular to the cut already made, or it may require a little soap applied to the teeth. If the ease of sawing does not improve, the teeth of the saw may require setting and sharpening. Any hardware shop will have this done at nominal cost. Keep the saw blade covered with a thin film of oil while it is not in use.

98 Planning and measurement without numbers

Identical rudiments apply to all crafts in making plans, drawings and measurements. Some of the tools used in carpentry make it possible for young people to plan and duplicate parts without using numerical measurements.

Tools: set square; right-angle triangle; compass; dividers; marking gauge; pencil; mitre box

A simple six-sided box can be made by a child who is not yet familiar with mathematical operations.

Materials: 60cm × 7·5cm × 2cm (24″ × 3″ × ¾″) wood; 30cm × 30cm × 6mm (12″ × 12″ × ¼″) plywood

The child marks off a short length of 7·5cm (3″) wide wood. He then places it inside his mitre box and cuts along this mark (see 97). He places the short, sawed-off piece on top of another, longer piece of 7·5cm (3″) wood, with ends lined up, and runs a sharp pencil point along the other end of the top piece, marking another of the same size on to the bottom one (see diagram). After this second piece is cut, he will have two identical pieces for opposite sides of the box. When the same operation is repeated a second time, the four pieces required for the frame of the box will be complete. He can glue, nail or screw these sides together, using corner clamps (see 90). This frame can then be traced on to the 30cm (12″) plywood

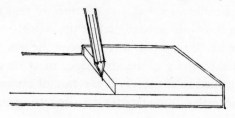

to form the bottom and lid of the box. After being cut with a saw, they can be glued, nailed, screwed or hinged to the frame. Use the marking gauge to indicate the line on the top and bottom pieces along which nails or screws are to be driven (see 100). The box will be reasonably square and a satisfying piece of work.

99 The set square

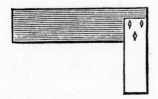

This tool is of value only if at least one side of the wood is perfectly straight. For younger children all sides of the wood should be trimmed square before it is given to them.

100 The marking gauge

This tool is especially useful at a stage at which the child cannot as yet make numerical measurements with precision.

He can set it to any desired width and duplicate this measurement elsewhere. For example, he can set the gauge to approximately half the width of the edge of a piece of wood and mark this distance on the top side of any other wood to which it is to be nailed or screwed. Nails or screws driven along such a line, unless they are driven crooked, are unlikely to protrude through the outside surface of the wood beneath.

101 Templates

Templates are useful in any craft, especially at an age when the child cannot measure with accuracy or where organic shapes defy measurement (see 65). Once a child knows how to make

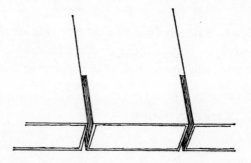

templates, he can duplicate or transfer any shape he wishes. Insist that the child invents his own templates. Point out that when a template is used, a pencil line drawn around the outside produces a slightly larger (and one drawn around an interior shape a slightly smaller) duplicate of the original. In sawing or otherwise cutting out such a shape an allowance must be made for the difference by cutting either slightly inside or outside the marked line, as appropriate, or redrawing it beforehand (see diagram).

102 Using tools to make tools

Braces, struts, temporary supports for pieces that are to be jointed, strips of wood fastened to the workbench to hold a board that is being worked on, and other temporary aids devised by the young craftsman are a sign of mature craftsmanship. Encourage the invention of tools that aid or speed

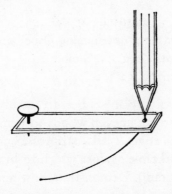

the work. For example, a strip of 1·25cm × 2·5cm × 30cm ($\frac{1}{2}$" × 1" × 12") wood into which holes, small enough to hold a pencil snugly, are drilled at intervals, and a nail driven through one end, can be turned into a useful beam compass (see diagram).

103 Jointing

Use of the mitre box (see 97) and corner clamps (see 90) gives the young craftsman ideas about jointing wood. Other, more complex and durable joints will enable him to use his craft with greater versatility.

104 Bracing

Wooden strips and right-angle and other braces can be glued, nailed or screwed to a wooden base to provide temporary or permanent support for other pieces that are attached to them and each other.

105 The plane

The plane is a sharp tool, and as such demands of the user considerable experience, coordination and self-discipline (see also 69).

Tools and materials: block or trimming plane; workbench (see 81); 5cm × 15cm × 35cm (2″ × 6″ × 14″) pine; 2·5cm × 5cm × 25cm (1″ × 2″ × 10″) pine

A block or trimming plane is best to teach young carpenters how to shave warped, uneven wood; to trim wood too thick to fit; or to round edges. Nail a strip of 2·5cm × 5cm (1″ × 2″) wood to the worktable against which to brace the wood for planing (see diagram). Demonstrate how and why the wood

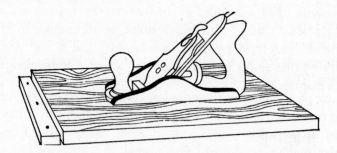

must always be planed with the grain, and how to adjust the blade setting at the knurled knob attached to the handle of the plane.

Check the depth of the cut by inspecting the knife edge on the bottom of the plane and try it out on scrap wood. A thin, level, even sliver, and no more, should be removed with each pass of the plane. Too deep a bite or a blade set crooked will nick and crease the surface so that it requires endless planing and sanding before it is smooth and level again.

106 Wood finishing

After a construction or an object has been made, the young
carpenter may choose to preserve the wood – paint, varnish,
shellac or stain it. Younger age groups will find it sufficiently
satisfying to paint wood with poster colours (see 149). If they
wish, they can protect the painted surfaces with water glass
(see 42), transparent glue (see 26) or a light coat of varnish
or shellac. Bear in mind that the last two are volatile and toxic,
and constitute a serious fire hazard. They also ruin paint
brushes unless these are thoroughly rinsed in a proper solvent
after use and then washed in warm water and soap (see 110
and 165).

107 Sanding and sealing wood

Tools and materials: sandpaper (in two or three different grades,
ranging from medium-coarse to fine); steel wool; sealer;
flat 2·5 cm (1″) paint brush (or wider if the work is large); rags

Wood should be sanded and sealed before it is painted, or most
of the paint will sink in, giving it an uneven coating. Sealing
compounds for wood are best bought in hardware and paint
shops. The wood should be thoroughly sanded, first using a
coarse paper and then finer grades, always with the grain, until
it is perfectly smooth to the touch. For a high finish it should
then be polished with fine steel wool. Two light coats of
sealer, each evenly applied with a brush, will close the pores of
the wood. The second coat is applied only after the first has
dried completely. Wipe away any excess with a cloth or rag
after each application. After the final coat has dried, rub it
down gently with steel wool once more.

108 Painting the wood

The variety of water- and oil-base and synthetic paints, enamels, and other finishes is so great that it would be futile to try to list and describe them. Dress the child in old and protective clothing. (See 11 and 165 for essential general safety precautions.)

If the construction or object is to be painted in a single colour, it is best to do so after final assembly of all parts. However, if small sections or parts are to be painted in several different colours or shades, it is best to paint them before assembly, provided no edges that are to be glued are covered with paint. Painted surfaces give poor adhesion.

109 Natural wood finish

Tools and materials: linseed oil; white (clear) vinegar; turpentine; rags

Mix all three liquid ingredients in equal proportion. Keep in a closed jar and shake well before using. After the wood has been sanded (see 107) but not sealed, apply this mixture to the surface with a cloth; wipe off any excess. Repeat this process two or three times, rubbing with steel wool after each application has dried, until the wood is thoroughly penetrated and the pores are sealed. This provides a matte finish that is resistant to water, alcohol and other stains.

110 Brushes

Use bristle brushes, 1·25 cm ($\frac{1}{2}$″) wide or wider, for painting wood, depending on the size of the object or the delicacy of the design. Use long-haired, narrow brushes for stripes, and round ones for painting detail. Instruct the young craftsman never to leave paint-filled brushes lying about but to rinse them at once after use, in the appropriate solvent.

Brushes on which paint has dried are difficult to restore, and may be totally ruined. Wipe the brush on newspaper or rags and rinse it in thinner poured into a jar. Then wash it in

mild soap and warm water. Brushes should never be stored standing on their hair. Keep them lying flat or standing on the wood handle in a jar, or, preferably, hang them by the handle so that none of the hair touches any surface. If paint has dried on a brush, it should be hung in solvent. Make a brush holder out of wire that allows the brush to soak without its hair touching the bottom or sides of the jar (see diagram).

4 Wire and metal

... This is an art
Which does mend nature – change it rather: but
The art itself is nature. *William Shakespeare*

111 Background

In early cultures that discovered the material and the means
to refine and work metal, the tribal smith or metal craftsman
was a man set apart from the rest. His secrets were sanctified

by ritual and custom. The metal smiths of Benin in Africa, who wrought magnificent bronzes, the artisans of ancient China, Mesopotamia, Greece, Rome and South America, were versed in metal craft even while the people of central and northern Europe and those east and west of the Ural Mountains had barely become aware of the existence and possibilities of these materials. North American Indians were still in the Stone Age at the time of the arrival of Europeans, despite rich mineral deposits close to the surface on their continent. Yet today there is hardly any tribe or group of human beings, no matter how isolated, that does not possess some idea of how to work and use metals.

Some of the common metals we take for granted, like aluminium, were discovered less than two hundred years ago. The French emperor Napoleon treasured aluminium more than gold and ordered a special set of tableware to be cast from this metal for his court. But many metals will soon become scarce once again at the present rate of wasteful consumption. Even scrap metals, many of them essential in the smelting of alloys, are now in short supply. Huge quantities of discarded metal are heaped daily on to rubbish dumps to rust and be irretrievably dissipated.

112 Work spaces
(See 10 and 81.)

113 Safety and developmental education
The development of metal craft skills should begin at early ages. Working with metal is actually less dangerous than many other crafts that are regarded as safe. At earliest ages a child needs no tools other than his or her fingers to bend and twist pipecleaners or plastic-covered wire. The sharp ends of such wire are easily covered with masking tape.

Metal foil has edges that are not much sharper than those

of paper. The young child must learn that they should be treated with care and that the foil can be folded or rolled to be perfectly safe. Metal and the required tools can't be worked by a child in whose hands they are unsafe – he just doesn't have the strength. Coat-hanger wire, for example, is very difficult to model. Ordinary pliers require relatively large hands and a firm grip.

First projects
114 Pipecleaners

Tools and materials: pipecleaners;
modelling clay or modelling dough (see 53, 117, 175 and 195)

As in all craft, the young beginner needs ample opportunities to play with the materials. It is sufficiently difficult and intriguing to discover how to bend pipecleaners into curves and angles; how to twist two or more strands together; how

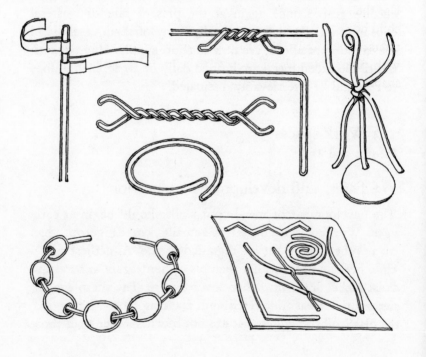

to splice several lengths; or how to insert one end of a pipe-cleaner into a lump of clay to make it stand up.

Other possibilities include gluing paper or ribbon to a pipe-cleaner; using pipecleaners as armatures for clay or modelling-compound objects, figures and shapes; stringing wood or clay beads on to pipecleaners; and pasting formed pipecleaners to card (see diagram).

115 Foil projects
(See 21–46.)

Wirework for beginners
116 Covered wire construction

Tools and materials: diagonal cutting pliers;
combination nose pliers; single-strand plastic-covered wire;
roll of masking tape; scissors

Use the same techniques as those described in 114. Show the child how to snip off required lengths of wire with the cutting pliers; how to bend, model and twist the strands by hand and with pliers. Dowels, cardboard tubes and other pre-formed shapes can be used as jigs (see diagram). As a precaution

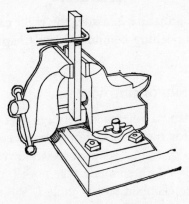

suggest that the child covers any wire that protrudes beyond the plastic-covered ends with small pieces of masking tape.

117 Making armatures

(See 53, 114, 116 and 195 for tools and materials.)

Any available wire that the child can work will do. For younger children pipecleaners are best as armatures for modelling with clay and dough. Older and stronger children can use coat-hanger wire (see 120–22). Sculptor's armature wire is available from art supply shops. It is fairly large in diameter but is made of soft, flexible, lightweight alloy that is easily cut with pliers.

Provide a 1·25–2cm ($\frac{1}{2}''$–$\frac{3}{4}''$) plywood base in which holes have been drilled (see 93), into which the armature wire ends can be inserted and secured. Or nail, screw and brace a dowel on the base to which the wire can be attached (see diagram).

Once the wire armature is made, the child can cover it with clay or other modelling compound (see Chapter 7).

118 The metalworking vice

There are substantial differences between a woodworking vice and one used for metalwork. For young people's craft purposes a metal vice can be adapted to woodwork (see 91), but not vice versa. For the beginner's wire modelling, a lightweight vice that can be clamped to any table is sufficient. For later, heavier work a vice, preferably one that swivels at least 180°, that can be bolted to a worktable is needed.

The vice is a practical, essential tool for safety. Materials held in the hand can slip and cause injury. Wire can be bent safely by hand or with a mallet when it is firmly locked into the jaws of a vice. Besides, most vices include a small anvil on the side away from the jaws that can serve as a wire modelling surface.

119 Wirework

Once the first metalworking skills, tools and experiences have been acquired, a child is ready for more advanced work. Wire modelling, apart from being an art form in itself, has many practical applications, from electric circuit wiring and repair to jewellery making.

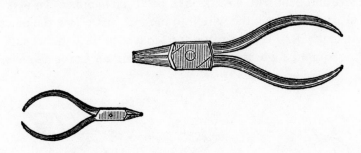

120 Wire cutting

Tools and materials: ordinary pliers;
diagonal cutting pliers (for cutting up to 22-gauge wire);
combination nose pliers;
hacksaw or jigsaw (for cutting 20-gauge or heavier wire);
metalworking vice (see 118)

Copper, steel and brass wire is available in different thicknesses, varying from 26-gauge (fine) to 12-gauge (heavy). It can be bought round, half-round and square.

Ordinary pliers can be used to cut wire, but they are not

very efficient, especially in the hands of young people. Even
diagonal cutting pliers will not cut heavy wire, like a coat-
hanger. Wire that cannot be cut easily with pliers must be
locked into the vice so that the place where the cut is to be
made protrudes slightly from the jaws. A half-round or triangular file (see 122), a hacksaw or a coping saw should be
used to cut heavy wire.

121 Twisting and jointing

Tools and materials: same as 120;
copper, brass or other soft alloy wire

The same basic twists, bends and joints apply as in 114. Wire
that is too difficult to model in the hand should be locked into
a vice and bent with a mallet or a ball peen hammer. To make
a sharp angle, lock the wire into the vice just below the place
where the bend is to be made and tap it with the hammer until
the required angle is formed (see diagram a). Curve the wire

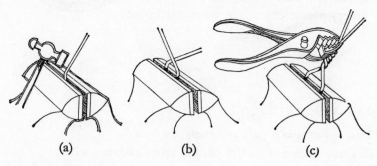

(a)   (b)   (c)

around pipe or dowel for round and oval shapes. To twist
heavy wires into a double strand, bend each at the centre into
a 45° angle and lock both pieces into the vice side by side (see
diagram b). Twist the protruding ends with ordinary pliers,
starting near the jaws of the vice (see diagram c), or use a
wrench if the wire is very heavy.

With these techniques wire can be bent and twisted into

interesting shapes. Start with copper wire that can be easily formed in the hand, twisted around itself or paper, cardboard or wood armatures (see 51–3 and 117).

122 Filing and finishing

Tools and materials: round metal file; half-round metal file; triangular file; needle file; steel wool; emery cloth or paper; buffing compound and cloth; metalworking vice (see 118)

Pliers (see 120) or files (see diagram) leave sharp, ragged ends on wire when used for cutting. Ends and edges must be blunted and rounded before the metal is worked. Heavy wire can be locked into the vice to file ends smooth and finish them with emery cloth or paper. Wire can be cleaned, polished or given texture or a high finish by rubbing with steel wool, emery paper, or buffing compound and cloth.

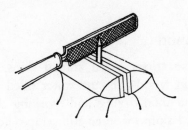

5 Leather

Never forget the material you are working with, and always try to use it for what it can do best. *William Morris*

123 Background

American Indian tribes cured animal skins by salting and burying them in wood-chip-and-water filled holes dug into the ground, and then drying and working them until they became pliable. Eskimo women still scrape and chew reindeer skins with their teeth to make them durable and soft enough for wearing. Tanning and tooling of leather were known among the Egyptians more than 1,300 years before Christ; in China this craft was perfected even earlier. The ancient Jews discovered how to preserve hides with oak bark, and they used leather for making ritual articles, sandals, leggings, and shields and armour, as did the Greeks and Romans.

Some of the first craft guilds were formed by British and European leatherworkers in the fourteenth century. Two different guilds became responsible for the preparation of animal skins – the tanners for leather and the skinners for furs.

Cutting, working and tooling leather take time and patience even when done by machine. But the ancient ways of working are still practised in Morocco, India and Mexico, and to a lesser extent by a few remaining European and American craftsmen.

Leather from various animal species has different thickness, texture and other characteristics. No leather made from other than domestic breeds should ever be used for craft. Split cowhide can be cut easily with scissors and worked by young children. Calfskin, sheepskin, pigskin and goatskin in various grades are obtainable from tanneries and craft suppliers. Suede is the flesh side of the leather regardless of its source.

Leather can be bought in whole and half skins, in sides, and as remnants. The back side of the skin is the most valuable, fault-free grade. It should be stored flat, grain side up, on an open shelf. Leather thong – thin strips of leather used for lacing and binding – is expensive. Vinyl lacing, while lacking the quality of the organic material, is a useful substitute, available from craft material suppliers.

The first efforts in leatherwork by children should be spontaneous and involve activities that familiarize them with the characteristics of the material and with the techniques and tools required to work it successfully. More mature young people should be encouraged to make paper templates and mock-ups (see 64 and 65) before working with the leather itself. Many of the paper and foil craft techniques – punching (see 18), lacing (see 20), weaving (see 42–6), scoring, scribing and cutting (see 37–41) – are essential preparations for leather craft. They involve similar, and in many cases identical, procedures, in less expensive, more easily worked, and expendable materials.

Beginning with leather
124 Scissors – cutting and gluing

Tools and materials: split leather (see 123); scissors;
sheets of heavy cardboard; leather glue; wax or tracing paper;
mallet

Leather is usually cut with a sharp knife. However, young
children can cut split leather with ordinary scissors. Split
leather scraps can often be obtained free or inexpensively from
manufacturers of wallets, purses and gloves.

Scissors-cut split leather can be glued to itself or to cardboard, wood, metal, felt and other materials. Cow gum is the
most commonly used and effective adhesive.

White vegetable, casein and acrylic glues are also used.
Cornflour paste (see 27) adheres leather especially well. Suggest that a minimum of glue is used for such pasting so that it
does not stain the leather. Brush two or three light coats of
the cornflour glue on both surfaces. Press the leather together
before the glue dries. Wipe off any excess with a damp cloth,
then place the leather between two pieces of wood larger than
the glued surfaces and hold them together with G-clamps (see
90) for half an hour or more, until the glue is completely dry.

125 Collage and appliqué

Tools and materials: same as 124; leather remnants;
scrap material

Split leather from different hides, or dyed in a variety of stains,
can be used for collages and assemblages (see 29, 30 and 89).
Cut into very small pieces, leather can be used as mosaic
modules (see 31 and 201); use the adhesives suggested in 124.
Appliqué consists of pasting smaller pieces of leather to a
larger piece.

126 Stamping and punching

Tools and materials: round drive punch; revolving punch;
one-pronged chisel; multiple-pronged chisel; dividers;
rawhide mallet;
25cm × 30cm × 2cm (10″ × 12″ × ¾″) wooden workboard;
leather remnants

The listed punches and chisels are required for basic leatherwork, though one of each suffices for beginners. Punching
holes into leather is the first step for all lacing (see 127), sewing (see 131), and studding and grommeting (see 130).
Demonstrate how a line is marked with a ruler and soft pencil
wherever the leather is to be laced, sewn or grommeted. After
marking with a pair of dividers the places on the line where
the holes are to be made (see diagram a), use a punch or chisel
of a size that matches the lace, thread or grommet to perforate
the leather (see diagram b). All punching dies, including the
revolving punch, can be hammered with a mallet.

Two different hole patterns are generally used for lacing
around the edges of leather. The first consists of holes punched
in a straight line (see diagram c, and diagrams b–d on pages
115–16). The second consists of alternate, staggered holes for

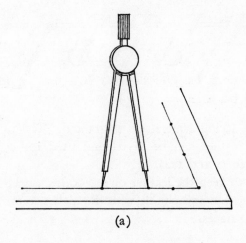

(a)

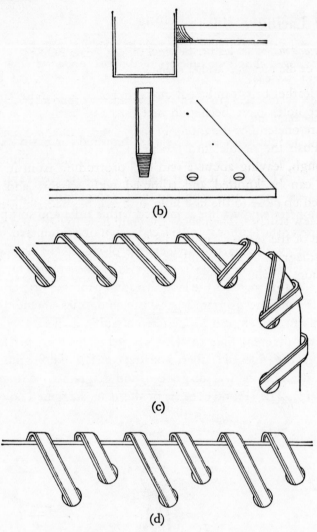

(b)

(c)

(d)

a different lacing effect (see diagram d). The punched-out circles of leather can be saved and used for collages and mosaics (see 31 and 124).

Be sure to keep the leather on a wooden workboard when driving punches and chisels with the mallet so as not to mar furniture surfaces.

127 Lacing

Tools and materials: leather or vinyl thong; lacing needle;
hole or die punched leather shapes

Old leather belts can be cut into thin strips to provide thong.
After holes have been punched into the leather (see 126),
secure one end of the thong in the lacing needle (see diagram
a). Push the needle into the first hole and pull the thong
through, leaving about 2·5cm (1″) protruding from it. This
end can be knotted and trimmed with scissors and then
pulled up close to the first hole, or it can be tucked under the
first few stitches. Then show the child how to lace around the
edge of the leather, from hole to hole, using the whipstitch
(see diagram b). If the holes are staggered, a more decorative
version of the whipstitch can be laced (see diagram d).

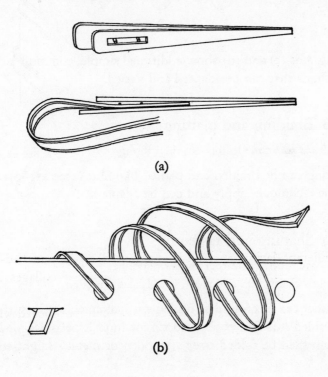

(a)

(b)

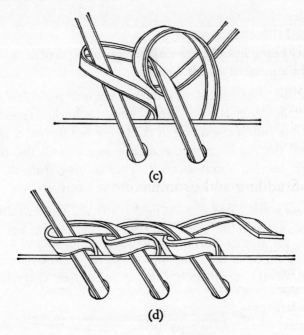

(c)

(d)

Diagrams (c) and (d) show additional simple, common lacing methods that can be adapted and varied.

128 Braiding and plaiting

Tools and materials: leather or vinyl thong

Thong can be braided and plaited like fibres (see 252–6); the same techniques apply and can be adapted.

129 Shaping and fastening

Tools and materials: leather; rags or sponge;
bowl of clear water and soap; towel; straight edge

Leather can be creased or folded without cracking the surface, provided it is first moistened slowly until it becomes pliable. It can then be folded over a wooden or metal straight edge.

Moisten the flesh side until the water begins to darken the finished side of the leather.

Very heavy leather, especially if it is to be carved or folded, should always be cased. This means scrubbing it clean with mild soap and water. Rinse off all soap and then let the leather soak in water for about five minutes. Wrap the wet leather in a towel and leave it overnight. Next day it will be soft enough to be worked.

130 Studding and grommeting

Tools and materials: same as 126; grommets and grommet die; eyelets and eyelet die; rivets and rivet set; rawhide mallet; 25cm × 30cm × 2cm (10″ × 12″ × ¾″) wooden workboard

Holes must be pre-punched for all of the above-listed fasteners and attachments (see 126), each the exact same size as or a shade larger than the diameter of the shank of the attachment. A variety of each kind is available, together with the required die or set, in craft supply shops. The metal piece is inserted into the hole and spread with the die and mallet (see 19).

131 Sewing

Tools and materials: leather; space marker wheel; or dividers; harness needle (for younger age groups or for heavy thread); 'sharps' (for older age groups or for finer thread); revolving leather punch; rawhide mallet; reel of saddler's or bookbinder's linen thread; or coarse nylon thread or twine

The harness needle is ideal for young children since it is blunt. 'Sharps' are available in various sizes. The line where the leather is to be sewn must first be marked (see 126), and spaces for stitch holes marked with the space marker wheel (see diagram a) or dividers (see 126) and then punched (see 126), before it can be sewn. Heavy leather to be sewn at the edges should be skived (the edge bevelled with a sharp knife) and if possible glued before marking, punching and sewing. The following stitches are those most commonly used in sewing leather:

Running stitch (diagram b)
Back stitch (diagram c)
Saddler's stitch (diagrams d and e)
Locked saddler's stitch (diagram f)

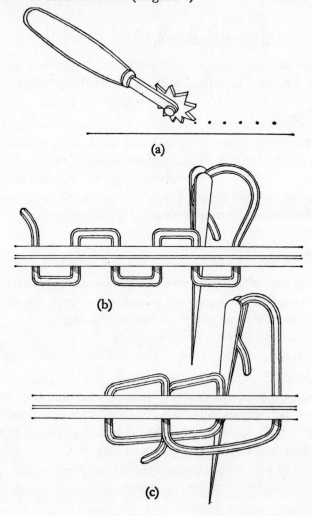

(a)

(b)

(c)

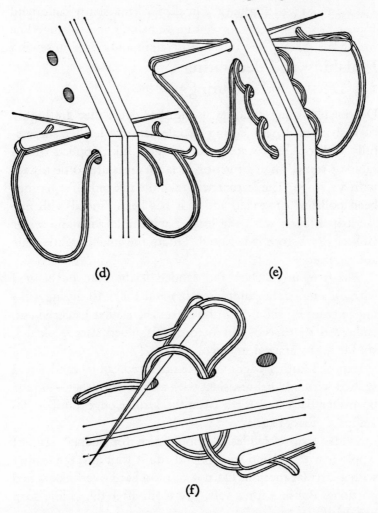

(d)

(e)

(f)

Awls for more advanced leather sewing are also available from craft supply shops and instructions are supplied.

132 Care of tools

Leatherworking tools, like all sharp tools, require frequent honing and occasional sharpening. They need to be kept rust-free and covered with a thin film of light oil, especially when not in use.

Finishing and decorating
133 Dyeing and colouring

Do not let young children use leather dyes; they are highly corrosive and toxic. Young people can dye leather successfully with ordinary waterproof or India inks, applied with a sable or camel's-hair brush or, if large areas are to be tinted, with a sponge. The leather will take the ink only if it has not been polished or waxed and if it has been sanded with fine sandpaper. First wash the leather with mild soap and water and let dry before it is tinted. Dilute the inks if subtle tints are required.

Wax-free, unpolished and sanded leather can be painted with oil and acrylic paints (see 167 and 168). All dyeing, tinting or painting should be done after the leather has been cut, embossed or carved, but before it is glued, laced, plaited, studded, grommeted or sewn.

Exposed leather edges that are not laced can be sanded and stained with ink or burnished with a bone burnisher. Rub the burnisher back and forth over the leather edge until it develops a glossy patina.

Saddle soap provides a good finish for stained leather. Apply it with a damp sponge and rub it well into the leather with a circular motion. Do not rub too hard over ink-stained portions. Polish with a soft, dry cloth after the saddle soap has dried.

134 Stamping and embossing

Tools and materials: leather; stamping dies;
embossing ball end modeller; rawhide mallet;
25cm × 30cm × 2cm (10″ × 12″ × ¾″) wooden workboard

Stamping, punching and embossing dies for leather are available in a great variety of designs. Provide only those that make simple geometric shapes – a circle, square, triangle, bar, or the like. A child can combine these to make designs.

Tape a scrap of leather to the wooden workboard, polished side facing up. Demonstrate how to hold the die in one hand and the mallet in the other, striking the flat, solid end of the punch to stamp the shape into the leather. Show how the different-shaped dies can be punched into the leather next to one another to form various designs. Embossing – engraving by pressing into the leather with a rounded modeller – is usually done on the flesh side of the leather.

135 Combining leather with other materials

The different leatherworking methods can be combined and used for work in other materials. For example, metal or wooden shapes can be covered with leather; leather shapes can be embedded into wood; and leather, fibres and fabrics can be combined in a number of creative ways.

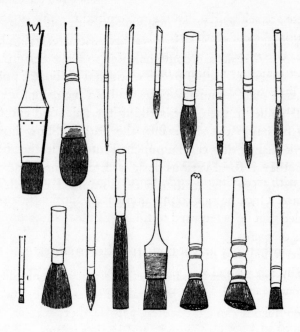

6 Drawing and painting

Art is a natural discipline. *Sir Herbert Edward Read*

136 Background

Drawing and painting are developmental necessities for children, just as speaking, reading, dancing, etc., are. A child needs art experiences, not to become an artist, but to exercise essential human qualities – coordination, vision, craft, imagination, thought and expression. A child who is given no free rein in the use of art materials, who is restricted to colouring books that speak for him or clay moulds that are pre-formed, who is told what to draw, paint, sculpt or mould, may never realize his graphic and plastic self-expressive faculties.

These are self-evident truths recognized in every branch of education – save in the art education of children or young people. Often they are violated at every turn. When the child uses art materials at home or in the classroom, he is usually given little opportunity to play with them or discover their properties. Instead he is often shown how to draw cliché clouds, ocean waves or people, smiling moons and suns, or the stereotype houses, trees, flowers and animals found in comic strips and TV cartoons. Or the child is given moulds to fill with modelling dough, or pre-drawn pictures to colour and trace. Once he can count, numbered outline pictures are provided that he is required to fill in with matching numbered pencils or paints.

Every child and every adult possesses a sense that is not generally recognized – a *sense of aesthetic necessity*. It dictates a preference, shared by our whole species, for a particular balance and order, symmetry and asymmetry, that, when experienced or created, evoke a deep sense of satisfaction. This sense of aesthetic necessity imbues human thought, language, music, science, mythology and art with a universality. At its highest cultivation it allows people from any culture to understand and appreciate all others. It embraces faith, belief and religious experience. In children this commonality lies closest to the surface of consciousness; it is not yet overlaid with cultural prejudice.

It is the dual responsibility of parent and teacher to introduce the child to his own culture and, at the same time, to nurture his universal sense of aesthetic necessity to protect him from cultural parochialism. The arts are one of the avenues by which these goals can be reached.

One cause of confusion in art education stems from a misunderstanding of the processes involved in learning how to write. Here the child must eventually draw symbols with accuracy. Yet early free drawing is an essential preparation for writing skills. The child can only learn to control his writing instrument by scribbling at random until his coordination increases to a point at which the pencil follows his dictates. Thereafter the child still needs freedom in his art, though for different reasons. The real purpose of writing is expression; but this exercise is denied the child while he learns his letters. Especially then, he needs free rein in his artistic activities.

Art should be a creative challenge, providing great satisfaction when it is met with whatever skill, ability, imagination and capacity for involvement the child possesses. Art activities create values. They educate the emotions and foster an ethical viewpoint. Forms and feelings can be tried out and their ethical implications explored without consequence. Art education provides a beneficial release of physical and psychological energy.

137 Chronology of development

No child should ever be made or expected to draw, paint or sculpt. Some children prefer other arts and crafts. But the materials should be made available and attractive to all children. The particulars suggested in this chapter match materials and techniques children can handle to a chronology of skill and perceptual development. Art interests and skills require encouragement. But even more than that, they require opportunity.

Some basics are worth observing. For example, crayons are easier to control than chalks; yet chalks are a more satisfactory medium. A compass is fun, but it should not be given to young children until they have enjoyed several years of free-hand drawing, or else the use of mechanical drawing instruments may become so attractive that they may preclude the development of other, more important skills.

As with all materials of play, the child's first efforts centre around an exploration of what the materials can be made to do and how he can affect and transform them. He must *play* with them. He increases his control through play. His abilities unfold in the act of discovery. The crayon scribbles turn bolder, into long, sweeping, involute lines, and then are converted into random dots and dashes. (By all means show the child that he can also lay the crayon on its side and, after peeling off the paper, make broad strokes and textured masses of colour.) The same principles hold true for chalk or paint, for squeezing, pressing and rolling clay into beads, sausages and flat sheets, or for scratching into dried slabs of modelling compound or plaster (see Chapter 7).

When he has exhausted the possibilities of spontaneous exploration, he may discover by accident that what he has drawn, painted or formed reminds him of a figure, animal, object or plant he has seen. The similarity between what he sees in his art and reality may be remote or nonexistent. 'Look! I've made a fire engine,' means no more than seeing a man in the moon. The child merely imagines or wishes that his creation is what he wants it to be. It is quite enough. It's a big step forward, but it's one that cannot be forced or accelerated.

Teach control of the material: 'Let's arrange all the paints over here, each jar with its tongue depressor to spoon out the paint into the bun tin. Dip out a little of each as you need it. But keep the paint jar lids closed so that the paint doesn't dry out. Also don't dip a tongue depressor or brush loaded with blue paint into the yellow by accident. It'll turn all the yellow paint green.' Suggest free experimentation: 'Make whatever you like. Try some big, long lines and then some very little ones.' Appreciate the result: 'That looks very good' (or happy, or sad, or rough, or smooth). Encourage discovery of the different effects possible with different materials. Suggest to the child that he tries out what happens when he rubs the paint with his fingers, or other tools that he chooses. Some techniques must first be demonstrated before a child can experiment with them on his own.

Ultimately the child begins to be able to predict what he is going to do with increasing certainty and sureness. The results may still seem unreal or abstract to adults, but they are very real to him. His main satisfaction stems from his ability to make tools and materials obey him.

Art teaches the child how to cope with failure. If something is messed up, it's easy enough to start over again, and improve with practice. Fear of failure (and refusal to try repeatedly once they have failed) is one of the major learning handicaps suffered by children in our success-driven time.

The child may suffer occasional frustration, especially at times when his understanding is ahead of his ability to express himself – as it usually is at all stages of development. But coming to grips with these frustrations and coping with them, instead of being frozen into passivity, is an essential lesson for every art and craft and for all of life. 'It is only fear that prevents the child from becoming an artist – fear that his private world of fantasy will seem ridiculous to the adult. . . . Cast out fear from the child, and you have then released all its potentialities for emotional growth and maturation.'*

As stated earlier, the child needs exposure to working artists and to the art of his own and other cultures and times. He can then become aware of the variety of forms and styles that is available. Reality and fantasy, filtered through his perceptions and limited only by the discipline imposed by physical circumstances, allow the child to create a *new* reality. This is what art is all about. Through his art the child participates in the real world – and at the same time he can invent his own, in which anything is possible, anything can be invoked or imagined.

* Herbert Read, *The Grass Roots of Art: Problems of Contemporary Art*, No 2, New York: Wittenborn & Co, 1947

138 Materials and work spaces

Every child needs his own private work space or, at the very least, room at a table low enough so that he can work comfortably, sitting or standing. He needs space to lay out his materials within reach. Preferably the working surface should be spillproof – Formica, linoleum, plastic, glass or oilcloth; or covered with protective material – a heavy sheet of cardboard, or layers of newspaper firmly taped down.

Children don't need an easel for painting. Most children's easels are too flimsy to be of any use. As an alternative work surface, layers of newspaper, a large sheet of cardboard or corrugated board, or a bulletin board, blackboard or wallboard can be tacked to, nailed to, or hung on a wall. The child then needs a tray hung below the wall work surface to hold paint jars, brushes, crayons or chalks, or a small table placed to his left or right, depending on his handedness. (See also 10.)

139 Surfaces

For drawing: newsprint; brown or white wrapping paper; greaseproof paper; white or coloured card; different strengths of cardboard; panels cut from corrugated cartons
For painting: all the above; sheets of printed newspaper; wallboard or plasterboard panels

Drawing and painting papers and surfaces should be large enough so that the child can make bold strokes with crayon or brush. This may seem wasteful, especially at early ages, when children tend to make a few scribbles on a sheet and then claim they have finished. But a pre-schooler can be encouraged to work all over the paper with some endurance if the paper is large enough and the supply limited.

Impress on the child that he must not draw or paint beyond

the paper surface on to wall, table or floor. Freedom has its limitations. It carries with it the responsibility to confine the work and to exercise essential restraints. Insist that the child helps to clean up after he has finished, until he or she is old enough to do this unaided. These are the right kind of controls – more beneficial than those imposed by staying within the lines of a colouring book.

Drawing
140 Crayon scribbling

Tools and materials: school grade crayons (see 139 for surfaces)

Children's wax crayons are available in a variety of grades. Provide only 'school grade' crayons. They are less brittle, larger, and more easily handled by young children than those usually found in toy, chain and stationery stores. Let the child experiment. (See 137 and 138 for additional suggestions on how to introduce him.)

At first, give the child a small assortment of primary colours only – red, yellow, blue, black, white. Add others later. Provide a box into which he can tumble them out of their packages; in the package they are too closely packed to be handled with ease. Keep each drawing session short, ending it as soon as the child tires. Keep paper and crayons on open shelves where he can reach them unaided. Don't set particular hours or days aside as drawing times. Rather suggest, from time to time, that he or she uses the materials in between other play activities.

Crayons are not an ideal drawing material. Chalks are much better. But the younger age groups can handle crayons more easily at first, without breaking or crumbling them as they work.

141 Chalk drawing on paper

Tools and materials: lecturer's coloured chalks
(see 139 for surfaces)

Large, fat lecturer's chalks are best. Show the child how to smudge colours chalked on the paper, with a rag, fingers or hand. Demonstrate some of the basic colour mixtures – blue and yellow, red and yellow, red and blue. Make the child aware of the three basic qualities of form – line, mass and texture (see 153); explain that 'texture' means both roughness and smoothness. (See 140 for other suggestions that apply to both the crayon and chalk media.)

142 Chalk drawing on a blackboard

Tools and materials: same as 141;
blackboard (see below for making your own);
felt blackboard wiper

Large slate blackboards are expensive. A satisfactory blackboard can be made by painting 'blackboard paint' on to well-sanded and sealed plywood (see 107). Apply several coats of the paint, each after the last has dried, using brush strokes at right angles to the preceding coating.

The advantage of a blackboard is that it is always in view once it has been hung. The picture can be wiped out and another started, without ever running out of drawing surfaces. But this is also a disadvantage: you cannot keep the result and hang it on a wall permanently. Children need to have their art admired and respected. They thrive on praise – it is an incentive for future work. Yet be discriminating. Once you have hung and admired some of the child's work, let him know that you prefer some of his drawings to others. Such criticism can be a spur to his future efforts.

143 Felt marker drawing

Tools and materials: small assortment of felt markers
(see 139 for surfaces)

Many felt markers are indelible. They contain dyes that, while non-toxic, discolour fabric and wood surfaces. Provide protective clothing and cover table and floor for beginners. Teach the child to replace the cap of each marker when he has finished using it for the moment, otherwise they dry out quickly.

Felt markers are available in a variety of nib sizes. Provide the child not only with a small variety of colours but also with different-size nibs, ranging from fine to broad. Suggest combinations of felt marker drawing with chalks and crayons. This increases variety of possible effects. (See 140 for other suggestions that apply to felt markers as well.)

144 Action drawing

Tools and materials: same as 140, 141 and 143;
large drawing surfaces (see 139)

Encourage movement with crayon, chalk and felt markers – broad sweeps made more or less at random across the paper. The child will then not get bogged down working in one small area of paper; he'll become aware of effects that might not otherwise occur to him. Suggest that he covers the whole paper or board with a single line that curves or zig-zags in and out and doubles back on itself, without lifting the drawing instrument off the paper.

145 Crayon transfer

Tools and materials: school grade crayons;
two or more sheets of bond (writing) paper;
large sheet of heavy cardboard (for working surface);
stylus; used-up ball point pen

Show the child how to cover one section of a sheet of paper with heavily applied wax crayon of one colour. Turn this coloured paper over on top of a second sheet. When the child draws on to the back of the heavily coloured area with a stylus, crayon lines will be transferred on to the second sheet.

Eventually the child may wish to draw several adjacent areas of colour on a new sheet of clean paper. When the paper is turned over and used as before, he will achieve surprising effects wherever one colour area changes to another. The position of the top sheet can also be varied so that different colours are superimposed in successive drawings with the stylus.

146 Crayon engraving

Tools and materials: same as 145

Show the child how to make a solid, thick area of a single light-toned crayon colour on one sheet of paper taped to the cardboard. Then cover this area with black crayon so that hardly any trace of the first colour shows through. Use the stylus to draw into the black area. As the child works, his design will show through the black in the colour that was applied first.

Two or more different light colours can be laid on top of one another and then covered with black crayon as before. Multicoloured lines will appear, depending on the amount of pressure applied to the stylus.

147 Mural drawing

Tools and materials: large sheet of wrapping paper tacked to a wall; crayons; chalks; felt markers

One child or a group of children will enjoy drawing a mural. Don't expect it to be completed in a single day – let this be a continuing project. Suggest that, in addition to drawing on to the paper, the children adhere cut paper (see 37–41), fabrics (see 272–4), and other scrap materials. Don't insist that the mural should be representational or assume any particular form.

First painting
148 Water painting

Tools and materials: large sheet of white or brown paper; bowl of clear water; long-handled, flat bristle brush

Young children need and enjoy water play. Painting with clear water, without colour, confines the mess and introduces the child to painting materials and techniques. A two- or three-year-old will get great satisfaction out of painting with water. No directions or safety precautions are required, save for a mop and a towel.

149 Poster paints

Tools and materials: red, yellow, blue and black powdered tempera pigment (available in packages from school and art supply shops); or the same assortment of ready-mixed poster paints in screw-top jars; long-handled, flat bristle brush; 225g (8 oz) glass screw-top jars; bun tin or paper cups; bucket, bowl or pail of clear water; tongue depressors or lolly sticks (to stir the paints); painting paper (see 139); newspaper or blotting paper; rags or sponge (for wiping hands and paint brush handle)

Powdered poster pigments are more economical than ready-mixed paints. Besides, they can be used for making finger paints (see 150) and other purposes. For brush painting, mix the pigments with water to the consistency of double cream, a sufficient quantity of each to fill one of the jars. Keep the lids tightly closed when the paints are not in use or else they'll dry out and cake. Distribute the different colours in the cups of the bun tin or paper cups for the child's painting, so that the whole batch is not ruined if he fails to rinse a brush loaded with one colour before dipping it into another.

Pre-mixed poster colours are equally useful, though more expensive. Do not buy fluorescent poster colours; they are toxic, though this fact is not marked on the label.

Dress the child in a plastic or other apron and roll up his sleeves before painting begins. Set up the paint and water containers within easy reach next to the paper or other work surface. Be sure to change the water when it gets muddy from repeated brush rinsing. Secure the paper firmly to the table or wall surface with masking tape.

Start the child at his first painting session with a single colour. When he has some experience in applying it to the paper, a second colour, a third, and more can be added to his palette. Once a second colour is provided, teach the child to rinse his brush thoroughly in water before dipping it into the different paint, or else he'll mix the colours inadvertently. Suggest that he mixes paints on his painting or in unfilled portions of the bun tin. Show him that, in addition to painting over other colours he has painted, he can paint one colour next to another. These are the first and essential disciplines required for painting. Accidents will happen; overlook them. You can guard against them by placing ample newspaper under and around the work.

Teach the child to thin out his paints whenever they get too thick (as they may). If he thins them too much you can always add a little more powder pigment.

Encourage the child to experiment – to try his brush in different ways, including the wooden end; to make lines, dots and solid shapes; even to use his fingers. Suggest large, bold strokes with the brush, as well as small, delicate ones. Then let him paint to his heart's content for as long as he enjoys daubing away.

When the painting is finished, help the child to remove it. Let it dry on newspaper or blotting paper, flat on the floor or table, before hanging it for display. Ask the child if he wants to paint another picture. Let him make the necessary preparations to whatever extent he is able and help him with the rest. At the end of a painting session, insist that he helps to clean up, screw the lids to the jars, wash out his brush and water container, and remove the protective newspaper from table and floor. The paint brush should be rinsed and then washed with mild soap and warm water. (See also 29, 30, 56, 153–5, 158, 159 and 160–64.)

150 Finger painting

Tools and materials: red, yellow, blue and black finger paints (see 152 for recipe to make your own); roll or sheets of finger painting paper (see 151 for alternative finger painting surfaces); four tongue depressors or lolly sticks;
two large bowls or buckets of fresh water; sponge or rags;
masking tape; newspaper or blotting paper; plastic-, metal- or formica-topped table
Finger paints are more difficult to use than poster paints – a fact not generally appreciated. Finger painting should follow, rather than precede, a child's introduction to painting with a brush (see 148 and 149). Separate one sheet of finger painting paper and tape it to the table surface. Set out the open paint jars, each with its own tongue depressor; the two bowls of water; and rags or sponge to one side and within easy reach, depending on the child's handedness. Spill a small quantity of fresh water on to the paper and distribute it with the palm of the hand or with the sponge until the paper is evenly moistened. Sponge away any excess moisture. Then dip out a small

blob of paint from one of the paint jars, using a tongue depressor. Spread the blob of paint on the paper with the palm of a hand. Then draw into the paint with a finger. Let the child work into the paint with his or her hands and fingers.

Provide the child with a single colour at first. Later a second, third and fourth colour can be added, each dipped out of its jar and dropped on to the paper as before. Show the child how to spread each colour *next to* the others on the paper, before mixing them in portions of the painting. This is important, or else each painting will turn out the same muddy purple or brown.

The disciplines of not mixing paints in their jars and not painting beyond the work surface (see 149) apply here as well, as do the guidelines concerning line, mass and texture effects (see 153). However, in finger painting some application beyond the paper is unavoidable as the child works up to and along the paper edge; this is why a washable table surface is essential.

Encourage experimentation with different effects the child can create, using his or her hands and fingers only. Suggest frequent washing of hands in one of the fresh water buckets or bowls to help keep the colours fresh. One of the advantages of finger painting is that, as long as paper and paints remain moist, a design can be wiped out and started again or changed. A few drops of water added when necessary will keep the paint and paper workable.

Once some of the hand and finger effects that are possible have been thoroughly explored in succeeding sessions, add a comb, dowels, wooden blocks and other materials to the child's inventory of work tools. He can draw these through the wet paint or press them into it, creating many different effects.

Let a finished painting dry on several layers of newspaper or sheets of blotting paper. If the painting buckles as it dries, it can be ironed between layers of newspaper or blotting paper. In succeeding painting sessions encourage the child to do as much of the preparatory work, paper wetting, and dipping out of paint as possible.

151 Alternative finger painting surfaces

If finger painting paper is not available, the following materials will take the paint adequately enough to permit the child to work in this medium:

Any slick, glossy paper, including the covers of magazines; a glass or enamel tray; a sheet of metal or foil; oilcloth

152 Making your own finger paints

Tools and materials: powdered poster pigments (see 149) – ½ tablespoon each of four colours; 1½ cups laundry starch 1 litre (2 pints) boiling water; ¼ cup talc (optional); four screw-top glass jars; 1½ cups soap flakes; tongue depressors, one for each colour

Mix the laundry starch with cold water to the consistency of a creamy paste. Add the boiling water and cook until the mixture becomes transparent and glassy. Stir constantly. Let the mixture cool somewhat before stirring in the soap flakes. Once these are completely dissolved, add the talc. Let the mixture cool and then pour it equally into the four jars, filling each to about an inch (2·5 cm) below the lip at most. Stir half a spoonful of each powder colour into its respective jar.

Soap flakes, liquid cornstarch, or wheat paste mixed with water to a creamy consistency can also be added to powdered pigments to make finger paints, depending on availability of materials.

153 Dot mass and line painting

Ask the child to paint with brush or finger (see 149 and 150) using dots or short dashes only. They can be placed closely next to one another or farther apart, or they can overlap. The same colour or different colours used in this manner will produce a great variety of effects when the finished painting is viewed from a distance. French pointillist painters at the turn of this century explored this technique with great imagination. Show your child black-and-white and colour reproductions of photographs, illustrations and paintings through a magnifying glass. He'll discover that all the different colours and shadings in printing are achieved through the use of small dots of only four colours, each printed next to the others. He can achieve similar effects with his dot paintings. The same can be done in drawings or paintings executed exclusively in line and/or in large masses of colour.

154 Line and blob blowing

Tools and materials: drinking straws;
liquid watercolours or inks; eyedroppers, one for each colour;
sheets of white drawing or bond paper

Many effects in drawing and painting are accidental. Once discovered, an artist can re-create them at will. This quality of art makes it playful and, therefore, of special value to children and young people.

Tape the drawing paper to a newspaper- or cardboard-covered tabletop. Use one of the eyedroppers to drop a small amount of ink or watercolour on to the paper. Show the child how he can 'chase' the colour across the paper by blowing at it with a drinking straw. Hold the straw while blowing so that it comes close to, but does not touch, the paint or ink. Different colours when blown in this manner can be used to create delightful effects and designs.

155 Blot pictures

Tools and materials: same as 154, omitting drinking straws

Fold a sheet of bond paper in half and then unfold it. Drop a small amount of ink or watercolour into the crease with an eyedropper. Now refold the paper and rub a finger along the crease without exerting pressure. When the paper is unfolded, a complex blot design will appear. Some control can be exercised, depending on where the ink is placed and how much pressure is exerted after the paper is folded. The variety of designs is as infinite as cloud formations.

156 Spatter painting

Tools and materials: old, discarded toothbrush, or stipple brush; poster colours (see 149);
watercolour paints or India ink in different colours (optional);
drawing or bond paper

Poster paints should be diluted to the consistency of single cream; liquid watercolours or India inks can be used undiluted.

Attach the paper to a wall (see 139). Load the toothbrush or stipple brush with paint. Then, holding the brush as shown (see diagram a), run a thumb over the tops of the bristles so that the paint spatters on to the paper. Different colours spattered next to or over one another, or one or more suc-

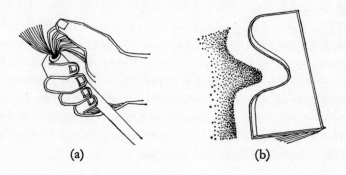

(a)   (b)

cessive colours spattered past a straight or shaped piece of paper or cardboard (see diagram b), will create a variety of effects. The various colour effects and mixtures will be similar in some respects to those possible with pointillist painting (see 153). The spatter technique, used by itself or in combination with others, can suggest forms, textures and designs that are limited in their variety only by the child's inventiveness and imagination.

157 Comb painting

Tools and materials: same as 149 and 150; an old comb

A comb drawn across wet poster or finger paint can create different line patterns. Parallel straight, wavy and crossed lines, and stipples (dots) made by moving the comb's teeth rapidly up and down on the paint, supply textures and increase the child's arsenal of possible effects. But more than this, such use of materials can stimulate the child to discover and create other, different effects.

158 String painting

Tools and materials: poster colours (see 149);
transparent watercolours or inks;
different lengths of string, twine or thread; sheets of bond paper;
newspaper-covered or washable table surface

Dip one length of string into one of the paint jars or ink bottles. Then lay the wet coloured string on to one of the sheets of paper and pull the string to form coloured lines and smeared areas of colour. When the first colour has dried, or even while it is still wet, draw another, differently coloured piece of string across the page, and a third if desired.

Or, the paper can be folded in half as for blot painting (see 155). Place and draw the coloured string through the folded paper.

159 Painting on wet paper

Tools and materials: same as 149; India inks or watercolours

When paper is thoroughly moistened and the excess water wiped off prior to painting on to it with poster paints, the colour, once applied, will run and spread in surprising ways. It will seep across the paper surface and blend into any other colour applied subsequently if the paper remains moist. The paper should be placed on a flat, level surface. If the child picks the paper up while the paint is still wet, he can make the paint run in whatever direction he chooses, and exercise some control over its spread and mixture. India ink, black and in colours, or watercolours, can also be dropped on to the wet paper and paint (see 154). These don't mix readily with poster paint; hence they will run over and around the poster paint and will dry in interesting patterns.

160 Action painting

Tools and materials: same as 149 or 150

See 144 for a discussion of purpose. Some caution is required so that the child does not splash paint, helter-skelter, beyond the painting surface. But it is important to encourage sweeping brush strokes.

161 Scrap materials painting

Tools and materials: same as 149; scrap materials

Natural and fabricated materials – egg cartons, cardboard, wood scraps, feathers, pebbles, paper cups and plates, egg shells, boxes – can be painted, decorated or used as the basis for a variety of art experiences. Suggest that the child designs with the materials, rather than just coating them with paint. The shapes and divisions of sundry packaging materials can in themselves suggest patterns and colour areas. (See also 29, 30 and 56.)

162 Mixed-media painting

After a child has had some experience with different drawing and painting media, he can combine some of these for a variety of effects. As discussed in 159 and in the various sections that deal with 'resist' techniques (see 166), even and sometimes especially those media that do not mix naturally offer opportunities for creating interesting effects when they are combined. Encourage the child to experiment – to invent techniques and to apply them imaginatively. He will eventually transfer the versatility of approach he learns in art to all his other activities.

163 Communal painting

Tools and materials: large sheet of brown wrapping or white paper taped to the wall; poster colours and brushes (see 149); one brush per child; bun tins, one per child; buckets of clean water

Several children can be encouraged to paint a communal design or picture. Each child can be assigned his own area in which to paint whatever he or she pleases. Or all children can agree to one common theme, each assuming responsibility for particular portions, shapes, colours or subjects (see 147).

164 Painting on dry clay, modelling dough or plaster

Tools and materials: same as 174–6, 189 and 192; poster colours (see 149); round bristle brush; shellac and solvent (see 165)

Clay, modelling dough or plaster, when dry, can be painted with poster colours by pre-school and older children. The painted shapes will not be waterproof and the paint is likely to flake off or stain fingers when handled. Do not bake or fire water-base-painted clay shapes – the paint will blister and discolour. To preserve such shapes after they have been painted, cover them with several light coats of shellac, each applied after the last has dried completely.

Shellac coatings should be applied only by adults and by mature young people able to observe the required precautions.

Advanced drawing and painting
165 A note of caution

The media and techniques detailed in the following sections are suggested for young people nine years old or older, depending on their experience, maturity, dexterity and interests. Some of these media require considerable caution (see also 11, 108, 133 and 164). Paints, other than water-based, casein and acrylic, and their solvents, are often highly toxic and in-flammable chemicals. Some contain high concentrations of lead that can cause brain damage if inhaled or ingested even in small quantities over a period of time. All the solvents for oil-base paints, japan colours, varnish, shellac, and model-making and plastic paints – turpentine, alcohol and acetone – can injure eyes and cause severe lung and skin irritation, especially when they come into contact with broken or sensitive areas. If that should happen by accident, or if any of these paints, or flakes of dried paint, or solvents are swallowed by a baby or child, contact your local hospital immediately for information about instant antidotes and remedies. As these paints and solvents are inflammable, they should only be used in well-ventilated rooms or workshops.

All such volatile, inflammable and toxic substances require great care in handling, protective clothing, gloves, and, if used over long periods of time, inhalator face masks. They should be stored in their proper closed containers, well away from other inflammable materials – preferably in a paint shed outside and away from living quarters or work areas. Read and heed the instructions and warnings on paint can labels before buying and allowing young people to use them. Some, like fluorescent colours, are toxic even though their manufacturers are not required by law to state this fact on the label.

Never allow children and young people to use aerosol spray paints, fixatives or, for that matter, any pressurized spray product. All chemicals inhaled as fragmented particles, and especially paints, are damaging since they coat the lungs. Never permit an empty spray can to be tossed into a fire or furnace – it will explode.

Transparent watercolours, though perfectly harmless, and pastel chalks, are unsuitable art media for children and young people. Paintboxes, usually sold as children's art materials, which contain small, dried cakes of paint that must be moistened with a brush are especially frustrating and useless, except to professional artists.

166 Wax crayon resist

Tools and materials: coloured wax crayons (see 140);
poster colours and bristle brush (see 149); or India inks;
bun tin (to hold paints); white drawing paper

Draw lines, masses, dots, textures and designs or pictures on to the paper with coloured wax crayons. Then, using poster paint thinned so that it flows like watercolour, or India ink, paint over the whole sheet of paper in one or several colours. The water-base ink or paint will flow into all the areas that have not been covered with wax crayons and in some places will be separated from the crayon designs by a fine white line. This combination of media that resist one another can be varied. For example, use only white crayon to make the drawings and paint over them with different-coloured paints or inks. The white drawings and textures will show up in sharp contrast to the paint.

167 Painting with acrylics

Acrylics are a relatively recently developed synthetic painting medium. They are non-toxic, water soluble, but they dry as a waterproof film. They can be applied thick, like oil paints; or in flat tones, like oil, tempera, or casein colours; or transparent, like oil tints; or in washes, like watercolours, depending on the degree of dilution. Acrylics are available that give a matte or a glossy finish, which does not yellow with time and requires no varnish or other protective coating. In addition to a standard assortment of colours, colourless acrylic preparations are available that can be mixed with paint pigments to increase or retard drying time, to make them more or less glossy, to give them more body or texture, as waterproofing over any other surface or paint, or as an adhesive (see 28, 57 and 164).

168 Oil painting

Oil painting is relatively slow, difficult to control, and painstaking, especially for younger children. It should not be attempted except by young people who have a great deal of experience in water-base media and acrylics, which are much more immediate since they dry within minutes.

169 Inlay cardboard painting

Tools and materials: poster colours (see 149);
sheets of heavy and light cardboard;
backing or drawing or writing pads; or corrugated board;
cardboard cutting and pasting materials (see 23–30 and 67–72)

Design and build a cardboard collage or assemblage and paint different portions to enhance the design and the three-dimensional effect. Contrast of dark against light tones, such as painting two adjacent sides or edges a light shade and the

other or others a darker shade of the same colour, will give
the construction greater depth and interest.

170 Sand painting

Tools and materials: sifted fine sand;
vegetable colouring or poster paints (see 149);
screw-top jars, one for each colour;
paper cones, one for each colour; scissors; masking tape;
white paste or glue (see 25–6); 2·5cm (1″) house painter's brush;
sheet of cardboard or brown wrapping paper; newspaper

Fill each jar about three-quarters full of sand. Then add
sufficient colouring to stain the grains of sand thoroughly,
using a different colour for each jar. Close and shake each
container to assure even penetration of the colour. Then pour

the coloured sand from each container on to a separate sheet
of newspaper; spread the sand and let it dry. Rinse and clean
all jars and let them dry. Pour each batch of coloured sand
back into its jar as soon as it has dried.

One painting cone is required for each separate colour. Cut
a small hole into the end of each cone, tape it closed, and fill
the cone with the sand. (If necessary, enlarge the hole until
the sand can flow freely; see diagram.) Fold over the top of
each cone and arrange all on the table, ready for painting.

Now brush the cardboard or wrapping paper with a thick coating of glue. Pick up one of the painting cones loaded with coloured sand, being sure to keep the tape adhered to the hole to prevent the sand from running out prematurely. Remove the tape and let the sand run out of the cone on to the paste-covered board or paper, moving the cone to make different shapes, lines, patterns and designs. Use the different painting cones to achieve a variety of effects, bearing in mind that the sand will adhere only as long as the paste remains moist. For this reason, it is important to use a good deal of very moist paste at the start and to paint rapidly with the sand cones.

To form solid areas of colour, outline the area with sand and then move the cone back and forth to cover the area evenly. Keep in mind that the sand will not adhere to itself but only to the exposed glue-covered area. When the design is finished or the glue has dried so that no more sand will adhere, let the painting stand and dry thoroughly for a while. Then, holding the painting over a waste basket or sheet of newspaper, shake off the excess sand that is bound to have accumulated but not adhered in some portions.

171 Painting on plastics

Water-base and oil-base paints, enamels and other conventional paints, inks and dyes do not adhere well to any of the common varieties except foamed plastics like polystyrene. They require special paints and solvents, all of which are toxic. (See 11 and 165 before providing young people with any of these.)

7 Pottery and modelling

Art is both a form for communication and a means of expression of feeling which ought to permeate the whole curriculum and the whole life of the school. A society which neglects or despises it is dangerously sick. It affects or should affect, all aspects of our life from the design of commonplace articles of everyday life to the highest form of individual expression. *The Plowden Report*

172 Background

The craft of pottery is more than seven thousand years old. Decorated pot sherds have been unearthed in Iran that date back more than five thousand years. The earliest potters formed clay found next to river banks and in swamps. Using the same methods described in 184-8, they worked the material, which, when dried for a period in the shade, provided them with storage vessels for grain and other dry solids.

Air-dried and unfired natural clay pots are easily broken; they cannot be used for cooking since they crack when heated over an open fire. Liquids can seep through the pores of the clay. Prehistoric craftsmen discovered that slow heating and cooling hardens clay that is free of air bubbles, and makes it impervious. Some of the impurities left in the clay, like fine silica sand or even soot from the fire, provided accidental, primitive glazes that strengthened and waterproofed the vessels further. By about 1500 BC the Egyptians and the Chinese had independently produced highly colourful and successful glazes. Those used by the Egyptians were eventually adopted by the Greeks and Romans. A great variety of glazes have been developed since, most of them lead-based, that provide durable and decorative finishes for different ceramics.

In ancient Crete, Egypt and Greece, as in China and South America, succeeding generations of potters contributed innovative techniques and styles, leaving distinctive marks on their pottery. Classic earthenware forms evolved, based on utility and convenience but also on what was pleasing to eye and hand, and these were eventually sanctified by ritual and custom. Bands of colour made of tinted 'slip' – watered-down clay – and glazes coloured with earth and vegetable dyes were added. Later artists drew designs and pictures on vessels with these colouring materials. Still others built up designs in relief, using slip as a modelling compound or adhesive.

Incising into clay led to the development of the alphabet. At first pictures were drawn on moist slabs of clay. In time these turned into a kind of shorthand that evolved into cuneiform, the early writing of Mesopotamian civilizations. Writing in cuneiform meant pressing wedge-shaped tools into moist clay, each wedge or combination of wedges standing for a different word or idea. Early in the first century AD the Chinese discovered that incised clay tablets could be inked and the design or picture transferred to paper by rubbing to make multiple copies (see 13 and 202). Thus ceramics played a crucial role in the discovery of printing.

Sculpting and carving in stone are related to forming with clay as well as to the bone and flint chipping of Stone Age civilizations. Prehistoric societies like those of the North American Indians learned how to flake chips off flint, using other stones as tools. Animal bones, soapstone, soft sandstone, limestone and alabaster were eventually worked in different cultures for utilitarian, decorative, architectural and ritual purposes. Once iron was mined and formed (see 111), harder and more durable stone like marble could be worked with metal tools. And with the discovery of casting techniques and materials, clay came into wide use in sculpture again since clay-formed objects could be duplicated in plaster of Paris – a form of powdered alabaster – and in bronze and other metals.

Mosaic craft is included in this chapter, though mosaic tiles are traditionally made of glass. Glass mosaic tiles are too difficult and hazardous for young craftsmen to make and cut. Commercial glass tiles are available, but it seems more productive to encourage young people to make their own tiles out of clay or plaster. (See also 31.)

173 Pottery and modelling for beginners

In pottery and modelling, more than in other arts and crafts, it is useful for young children and even older ones to gain experience in a particular chronological order. First they need experience in forming with clay or modelling compounds spontaneously so that they can discover their qualities.

Clay is delicate. Learning to wedge clay as a matter of course (see 178 and 191) will assure the young craftsman that his creations will not crack while drying or being fired. Attaching components of pottery or sculptures with slip (see 179 and 193) assures that they won't drop off as the clay dries.

Evading these simple disciplines leads to disappointment. The work becomes increasingly satisfying and productive if these and other operations become second nature.

174 Commercial modelling compounds

There are any number of modelling compounds other than natural clay available from art and craft supplies and toy shops. Some are claylike or clay derivatives that dry impervious without firing. Many of these can be painted with poster paints (see 149), acrylics (see 167) and other media. Many are useful for children and young people.

Some modelling compounds, like Plasticine, retain their malleability indefinitely and never dry out. They are not recommended for use by children. Other synthetic modelling compounds, like plastic wood and metal, are highly toxic.

Commercially available modelling 'dough' is a good working material for young children, though expensive, considering that it can be made at home or in the classroom at practically no expense.

175 Homemade modelling compounds

(a) *Modelling dough (I)*

Tools and materials: 2 cups plain flour; 2 tablespoons olive oil; small plastic bags and string; cold water; 1 cup salt; vegetable colours

Mix flour, olive oil and salt until they are uniformly distributed. Add water until the dough is stiff without being sticky. Divide the dough into as many parts as the number of different vegetable colours that are available. Press a thumb into each lump of dough and pour a few drops of vegetable colour into the dent made. Then work the colour evenly into each lump and place it in its own plastic bag. If the bag is kept closed in the refrigerator, the dough remains usable for three to four days. Periodic moistening and working of the dough will keep it fresh and workable for a longer time. The dough can be made without olive oil, using equal proportions of flour and salt, diluted with water only.

(b) *Modelling dough (II)*

Tools and materials: 1 cup salt; saucepan; vegetable colours; ½ cup boiling water; ½ cup cornstarch; plastic bags and string

Stir salt, cornstarch and water over low flame until stiff. When cool, knead until the dough reaches a pliable, even consistency. Add vegetable colours and store as described in 175a.

(c) *Wood dough*

Tools and materials: 1 cup sawdust; ½ cup flour paste (see 25); cold water; plastic bags and string

Mix ingredients and knead dough until it becomes uniformly pliable. Store as in 175a.

176 Clay and clay storage

There are three basic types of clay: earthenware clay bodies, stoneware clay bodies and porcelain clay bodies. All are found in different colours, each containing different minerals. Stoneware clay is best for young craftsmen. It is available in grey and in a reddish-brick colour (terracotta). Other clays vary in colour, ranging from black or white to various shades of grey and brown.

Clay is best kept in a metal can with a tight-fitting cover, like a rubbish bin. Place three bricks in the bottom and cover them with a wooden board. Add clear water up to just below the level of the board. Then place lumps of moist clay on the board and cover them with canvas or other rags, leaving an end hanging in the water to act as a wick, drawing up water as needed to keep cloths and clay moist (see diagram). Add another layer of lumps of clay, wrap the cloth over them, and so on until the can is filled to a level where the cover fits snugly. As long as water is kept in the bottom of the can and

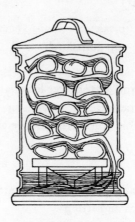

the cloth is kept moist the clay will remain soft and workable indefinitely.

Clay that has been permitted to become too dry to be workable can be reconditioned; wait until it is completely dry and hard. Then place large chunks in a canvas bag and break them up with a hammer or mallet. Sift out the powdered clay and keep hammering the large lumps until they are reduced to very small pieces, granules and powder. Place the dry clay particles in a metal can and cover them with several inches of water. Let stand for a week or longer, until the clay has turned uniformly mushy and no granules remain. Pour off excess water. Let the clay stand for several more days and then pour off whatever water has settled on top. The clay is now reconditioned though still too moist to be workable. Remove portions as needed and set them on to a plaster bat (see 192). The excess moisture will be absorbed by the plaster within one half to one hour; then the clay is ready for wedging (see 178 and 191) and use.

Clay should be soft, yet firm for pottery, and somewhat stiffer for modelling and sculpting.

177 Work spaces

For work with clay and modelling compounds, a child should be dressed in old clothes, in a smock or an apron. Sleeves should be rolled above the elbows.

Provide a table at which the child can work in comfort, standing or sitting (see 10). He or she also needs a sheet of heavy cardboard or plywood, approximately $35\,cm \times 42\,cm \times 3\,mm$ ($14'' \times 17'' \times \frac{1}{8}''$), as a work surface. Cover the rest of the table with oilcloth or newspaper. A bowl of slip (see 179), a bucket of water, and a towel or rags should be available to wash and dry hands periodically.

178 Working up and drying clay

Get the child used to wedging clay before using it for pottery or modelling. It is unlikely that he or she can do this properly at an early age, since it requires a good deal of strength and perseverance. (For more craftsmanlike wedging, see 191.) Until the child is more mature, encourage him to break the amount of clay needed for a project in half repeatedly and press and beat both portions together again to work out as many air bubbles as possible. Clay that contains air bubbles may crack even while drying in air and especially when fired in a kiln.

Allow the finished work to dry thoroughly at room temperature for at least two to three days. If this 'greenware' suffers any flaw – air bubbles; walls too thin; clay or dough too dry while it was worked so that it cracks; or added parts fall off because they were improperly adhered to the main body (see 182) – it can be repaired with slip (see 179). Discuss possible reasons for these flaws with the child and encourage him to avoid them in future work. Works that dry more or less properly deserve ample praise and prominent display.

Pinched, coiled and slab-built pottery or sculpture can be bisque-fired in a kiln (see 194) and glazed (see 194) if: the proper clay was used; it was properly wedged; coils and slabs were properly joined with slip; and the pottery or sculpture was thoroughly air-dried. It is unlikely that young children can keep all this in mind, even under supervision. Their work is therefore best left unfired, though it can be painted once it is thoroughly dry (see 164).

Modelling doughs cannot be fired, of course. When dry they can also be painted (see 175), preserved, and waterproofed to some extent with several coats of acrylic medium (see 167), transparent glue (see 26), shellac, clear varnish or nail polish (see 165). The same is true for self-setting clays.

179 Slip

Slip is required for successful clay or pottery work. It consists of clay thinned with water to the consistency of double cream so that it can be applied with a brush. Slip can be used to smooth out rough or jointed portions of clay, cement coils and slabs (see 185, 186 and 188), or fill cracks that appear as the clay is worked into shape. (Filling cracks is not recommended for clay that is to be fired.) Slip is also the required adhesive for attaching small parts to the main body of the work – arms to a clay figure, a handle to a cup, or other formed details and decorations.

Keep the bowl of slip next to the child and get him used to working with it as with the regular clay.

180 Drying finished work

Unfinished work can be kept workable as long as required by covering it with a damp cloth. Be sure to keep moistening the cloth periodically. Once the object is completed it must be air-dried, whether or not it is to be glazed or fired. It is important that the object dries as evenly as possible. Cover small extensions or additions to the main body of the work with dry cloths or rags to retard the rate of drying out of these portions. Due to the usually thinner wall thickness of handles, spouts and other small added parts, they tend to dry more rapidly than the rest and may crack, especially at slip-jointed edges. Once the rest of the vessel or shape has dried partially, the small additions should be uncovered so that they will dry along with the rest.

Keep a drying clay shape on a sheltered shelf, indoors, in the shade. Do not move it while drying and do not try to speed up the drying process. Clay shapes of average wall thickness take at least a week to dry out.

181 Basic forms

Sections 1–7 and 137 explain why a child should be encouraged to discover his or her own forms and shapes. But children also need to learn some of the basic processes to which the material lends itself and through which they can develop their own forms. In work with clay or modelling compounds these introductions are essential. Then let the child pinch, pull or pound the material to see what happens, combine and attach them to each other with slip or toothpicks and develop an endless variety of adaptations.

(a) Rolling beads

Break off a small lump of clay, about the size of an adult's fingernail or larger. Show the child how to roll it between his

palms to shape it into a roughly formed sphere and to continue rolling it with a circular motion of his palm on the table
or other work surface until it turns into a ball. Thread finished
balls on to toothpicks or a threader (see 17) and let them dry
completely. Perfectly round or slightly flattened beads can
then be painted, strung or used for mosaics (see 31 and 201).

(b) Rolling coils and strips

Break off as much clay or dough as fits comfortably into a
child's hand. Show him how to squeeze and then roll it
between his palms to form a sausage. Break off a small section
of the sausage and roll it between palm and table or workboard surface until it reaches the desired thickness. Keep
breaking off lengths for easier handling. The rest can be rolled
into coils later, and the coils can be flattened with a small strip
of wood if so desired. Keep the coils covered with a damp
cloth so they will stay moist until they are used.

(c) Forming a flat slab

Break off as much clay or dough as the child can hold comfortably in his or her hand. Place it on the working surface and
pound it more or less flat by hand. Place this roughly formed
slab between two strips of 6mm or 12mm ($\frac{1}{4}''$ or $\frac{1}{2}''$) lath,
depending on the thickness of clay slab required, and roll out
the clay or dough between the pieces of lath with a rolling pin

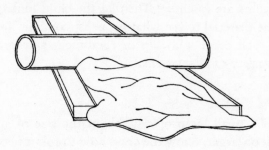

or bottle (see diagram). Be sure to keep the rolling pin or bottle on the lath. When the clay is rolled out to a uniform thickness, it can be cut into strips or other shapes with a dull knife edge or with cutters made out of strip metal. Such a slab can be used for pottery (see 188), sculpture and building. Patterns and textures can be drawn, etched or pressed into it.

182 Combining basic forms

The three basic clay modelling techniques can be modified and combined. The spherical beads (see 181a) can be rolled into ovals or, pinched in the centre, turned into bar-bell shapes, among others. The coil strips can be twisted into spirals or other curves (see diagram a), or the slabs can be folded back and forth to form accordion shapes (see diagram b). These and other variations can be combined, stuck to each other with slip or toothpicks while still moist, or used as decorative devices on pottery and other objects.

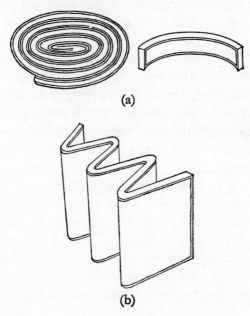

(a)

(b)

183 Textures

The moist clay can be scratched into with toothpick, wire or pointed tool. Short lengths of wooden dowel, children's wooden blocks, sanded scrap wood shapes (see 87), and bottle caps can be pressed into clay slabs to form patterns and designs. Plastic or wire mesh, rope, twine, embossed wall-paper scraps and any other textured material can be used. Don't neglect to point out that smoothness is a texture too. Show the child how to make slabs or shapes velvet smooth by brushing over the surface with slip (see 179). When dry, the smooth clay shapes can be polished with wax to heighten the effect. Textured clay slabs can be painted after they have dried (see 149 and 167).

184 Thumb pots

Give the child a small lump of clay, no more than fits com-fortably in his hand. Suggest that he wedges it (see 178) as well as he can. Let him form it into a more or less round or oval shape. Then demonstrate how he can press his thumb into the centre of the ball and smooth the inside and outside with slip (see 179). He's made his first thumb pot.

Once he has made several thumb pots, show the child how he can work on his next one with thumb and fingers to extend and thin the wall of the pot. Demonstrate how he must work all around, pressing the clay, a little at a time, so that the pot remains more or less round and the wall thins out evenly. He can smooth the inside and outside of his pot with slip, incise textures or designs on the outside, or add handles made from coil strips (see 181b) or slabs cut into strips (see 181c), using slip as an adhesive.

Other variations and refinements consist of squeezing a finished thumb pot into a number of pinched shapes; pressing a pouring lip into the rim; and adding a coil or slab-built rim or base. Don't insist on perfection, and do admire the result of the child's work.

185 Coil pots

Let the child make a number of coil strips and cover them with a damp cloth (see 181b). The base should be made out of a tightly wound coil (see 182) or out of a slab cut with the rim of a glass (see diagram a). Curl up the edge of the base all round and smooth it with slip. This is essential whether or not the coils of the pot are to remain visible, since the slip makes the coil strips adhere to each other and fills in small gaps that may not be visible.

Place the next coil all around the inside of the curled up base. Pinch off any extra length and pinch both ends of the formed coil so that they fit together to form a joint no thicker than the coil itself (see diagram b). Professional potters cut each end at matching 45° angles and fit them together with slip (see diagram c). Now add coil after coil, adhering each to the last with slip. To make the pot belly outward, attach each succeeding coil layer on top but towards the outside of the last, overlapping it by about one-half the thickness (see diagram d). To make the vessel narrower, attach coils to the inside of the previous strip in the same manner. It is better not to make the walls of a coiled vessel perfectly perpendicular. The coils work best when they overlap. After adhesion of three or four strips, go over all of them with slip: either smooth them out by working both clay and slip into an even wall, or, if the coil texture is to remain visible, use slip to provide an additional bond for the coils. In working the coil walls they can be thinned, flattened and given additional shape; they are then less likely to separate when drying.

Coil pots can have wide, narrow or multiple necks. If dressed with slip and smoothed on the outside, they can be incised and lined, and decorations can be added with beads,

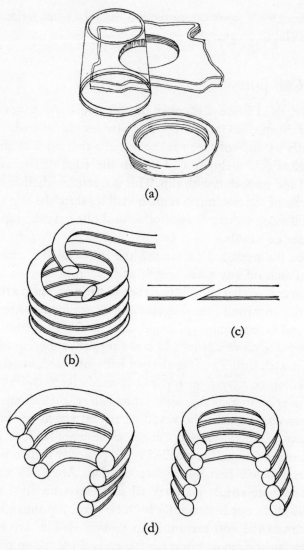

(a)

(b)

(c)

(d)

coil strips or slab strips adhered with slip. Handles, lips and stoppers can be added. There is no limit to the size of pots built with coils. Early Egyptian, Incan and African pottery was mostly coil-built and some of their vessels reached enormous size.

Slip-smoothed coil pots, when fully dry, can be decorated with coloured slip (see 193).

186 Coil sculpture

The technique described in 185 can be applied to sculpture. Simple and complex shapes can be built up with coils of clay. It's like building with logs, except that the clay coils can be bent and formed in any way desired. More experienced young people may need a basic assortment of sculpting tools to enable them to realize the possibilities offered by this method of modelling and building with clay.

Tools and materials: wedging wire (to cut off large chunks of clay); wedging board (see 191); knife (for cutting clay); sharp-pointed tool (for incising); modelling sticks; wire hook tools; sponge (for smoothing clay with water); brushes (for applying slip); syringe (for wetting clay surfaces); wet rags (for keeping clay moist); pail or bowl of fresh water

187 Hollowed-out pottery and sculpture

Solid clay forms take a long time to dry completely. It is therefore best to remove as much excess clay as possible from the interior of any formed shape without weakening the structure to the point that it collapses. Large, free-standing objects can be easily hollowed out through their bases, leaving at least a 1·25 cm ($\frac{1}{2}$″) wall. Some solid shapes, an egg for example, must be cut in half with the wedging wire. Scoop out the excess clay, leaving 1·25 cm ($\frac{1}{2}$″) wall, being careful not to squeeze or distort the outside shape while hollowing it. Fit the halves together and seal with slip. Correct any external distortion with clay and slip and let the hollowed-out egg air-dry on the shelf.

188 Slab-built pottery and sculpture

Using the technique described in 181c have the child form a 6mm- ($\frac{1}{4}$"-) thick slab of clay. Use a knife, wire or pointed tool to cut as large a square or rectangle of clay as possible out of the slab. Use a paper or cardboard template (see 65) or a right-angle triangle to assure that the slab is reasonably square. Now show the child how to lift the clay slab and form it into a cylinder, sealing the joint with slip (see diagram a). Stand this cylinder on another slab that is larger than the circumference of the opening and that has been thoroughly moistened with slip. Trim around the base of the cylinder with a sharp tool. Brush more slip into and around the joint, inside the vessel and out, to make sure of a good bond. A simple slab-built vessel has been formed.

Once the principle of slab-built pottery is understood, any number of shapes, vessels and constructions can be designed and modelled. Make a cardboard mock-up first; cut it apart and use the flattened cardboard as a template for the clay slab (see 65). Slab walls can also be set on a slab base and jointed by scooping out a small channel along the joint (see diagram b) and filling it in with slip and coil strips to form a good bond.

Slab-built pottery and sculptures can be built and draped around various forms or pressed into moulds (see 197). Fill a plastic bag with sand and drape a large slab of clay around it, joining the edges with slip. Use additional slabs to form the bottom and top, leaving a small opening. When the vessel or sculpture is almost a closed figure, puncture the plastic bag, let the sand run out, and pull out the plastic bag slowly through the opening (see diagrams c, d and e). Paper tubes, egg-carton bases, a blown-up balloon, a cigar box, a clay shape wrapped in newspaper, or any other object can be used, provided one end of the slab-built structure is left open enough so that whatever is used as the form can be with-

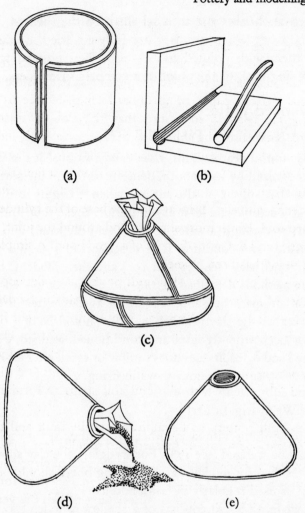

(a)　　　　　(b)

(c)

(d)　　　　　(e)

drawn. This opening can be sealed partially or entirely with an additional slab and with slip.

189 Engraving into dry clay slabs

Using the techniques described in 181c and 188, have the child prepare a number of clay slabs. He can cut them into whatever shapes he chooses and then set them on the shelf to dry for several days. When the slabs are fully air-dried, he can etch into them with pointed tools – a scriber, pointed wire or engraving tool, or the point of a compass or dividers.

Advanced pottery
190 Digging and preparing clay

Clay is found near streams, rivers and swamps. It can usually be recognized by its smooth, dense texture and the pattern of cracks that appear on the surface when it begins to dry out. Dig up a sample and let it dry in the air. Break it up and crush it, sift it through a sifter to remove grit, sand, and other impurities, and condition it as described in 176. Wedge the conditioned clay (see 178 and 191) and then model it by any of the methods described in 184–9. Let the completed object dry on an open shelf and, if a kiln is available, test-fire it to see whether the clay is suitable. More should be dug only if, having been properly sifted and conditioned, wedged, worked, formed and dried, it does not crumble or crack after air-drying or develop similar serious flaws in firing.

191 Wedging board

Before working with clay, either for pottery or for sculpture, it must be wedged (see 178). For wedging, the clay should be moister than for modelling. A wedging board should be built if clay is used regularly in fair amounts.

A wedging board consists of a shallow wooden tray to the rear of which a wooden post is attached; from the post wire is strung to one corner of the board. Clay is cut on the wire and wedged in the tray.

Tools and materials: 45cm × 60cm × 1cm (18″ × 24″ × ¾″) plywood; two strips of 43cm × 7·5cm × 1cm (17¼″ × 3″ × ¾″) pine; two strips of 60cm × 7·5cm × 1cm (24″ × 3″ × ¾″) pine; twenty-two 2cm (¾″) screws;

one strip of 6ocm × 2·5cm × 1·25cm (24″ × 1″ × ½″) pine;
one 75cm (30″) length of wire;
hand drill and bits; screwdriver; pliers

Assemble as shown in this diagram.

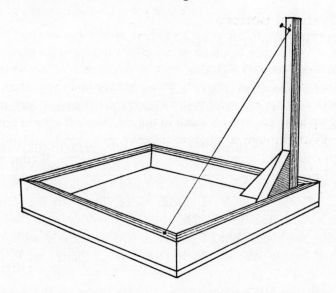

Scrape or break clay out of the storage bin (see 176), add
water if required, and work it into a solid lump. Then use the
wedging board wire to cut the lump of clay in half. Rejoin the
halves; turn one at right angles to the other and pound
together by beating and squeezing the clay by hand on the
wedging board. Repeat several times to be sure that all air
bubbles have been worked out of the clay and that it has a
uniform, moist and workable consistency. It will in all
likelihood be too moist and sticky for pottery or sculpture.
Place the clay on a plaster bat to remove excess moisture
quickly (see 192).

192 Making a plaster bat

Plaster that has set absorbs moisture. If you place wedged or other clay on a plaster bat – a slab of plaster – it loses moisture within thirty minutes to an hour, by which time it should be ready for pottery or sculpture (see 176). To make a plaster bat:

Tools and materials: plaster bat mould – a 15cm × 25cm × 5cm (6″ × 10″ × 2″) open box built of wood or a foil metal pie plate with about 5cm (2″) high rim;
2·5cm × 30cm × 6mm (1″ × 12″ × ¼″) sanded board;
2 litres (4 pints) plaster of Paris; 1 litre (2 pints) water (clear and cold); mixing bowl; large metal spoon

Sift the plaster slowly through your fingers into the water-filled bowl. Do not mix the plaster and water until all the plaster has been sifted and has formed a small mound about 5cm (2″) above the level of the water. Then stir the plaster slowly with the spoon. Do not remove the spoon while mixing the plaster but keep it immersed until the mixture has turned into a smooth, lump-free, creamy paste, ready for pouring. Pour the plaster into the plaster bat mould at once. Smooth the top surface of the plaster bat with the sanded board, if required. The plaster itself will set and be sufficiently hard to use within fifteen to thirty minutes. After it has set, tap the plaster bat out of its mould. Several bats should be made at one time. Each can be used repeatedly.

Place each lump of well-wedged but too moist clay on a plaster bat until it has lost enough moisture to be workable.

After work with plaster of Paris is completed, wait until the plaster has set and hardened in the bowl or on hands. Add water to the bowl, then rinse your hands in the bowl. The dried plaster will flake off easily. Drain the excess water through a sieve, collect the flaked plaster, wrap it in a newspaper, and burn. Plaster blocks drains.

193 Decorating clay with slip

Tools and materials: prepared slip (see 179);
poster paints (see 149); vegetable colours;
acrylic pigments (see 167); India inks; pottery or sculpture

Slip can be used to decorate sculpture or pottery that is to be air-dried, with or without kiln firing. If the clay is not to be fired in a kiln, coloured slip can be made by adding one of the pigments listed above to the slip.

If the clay product is to be fired, it is best to buy coloured slip of the same clay that was used to make the object, available in a variety of tints from art and craft supply shops.

Homemade or purchased slip can be painted on pottery or sculpture with water colour brushes. To paint even strips on a pot or vase, tie a flat lettering brush of the desired width to an upright stake (see diagram). Load it with slip, using another brush. The bowl, placed against the brush and turned slowly on the table, will receive an even stripe.

194 Firing in a homemade kiln

Before clay sculpture or pottery can be considered for firing it must be thoroughly air-dried (see 180). This takes a week or longer. Then, if it has not developed any flaws, the 'green-ware' is ready for its first, 'bisque' firing.

Kiln-firing is essential for any clay vessel that is expected to be durable and impervious to liquids, unless it is made of self-setting clay (see 174). A vessel can be glazed and fired at a first and only firing. Professional potters fire the unglazed clay during the bisque firing and then glaze it with a second 'glaze' firing. A single bisque firing, glazed or unglazed, is enough for young people's work.

Commercially available electric kilns, small or large, are expensive. The smallest ones severely limit the size of objects that can be made and fired. But it is possible to build and use a simple homemade kiln for unglazed bisque firing of pottery and hollowed-out sculpture.

Tools and materials: large metal rubbish bin with tight-fitting cover; spike or cold chisel and hammer;
enough sawdust to fill the rubbish bin;
sufficient coal or coke to line the bottom of the rubbish bin about 5cm (2″) deep; newspaper; air-dried pottery or sculpture

Use the hammer and spike (or cold chisel) to punch holes into the sides and lid of the rubbish bin, each 6mm to 1cm (¼″ to ⅜″) wide and about 7·5cm (3″) from the next. Line the bottom of the bin with coal or coke and place the largest air-dried pottery or sculpture on this layer (see diagram). Fill all spaces in and around the object and coal with tamped-down sawdust. Add a layer of 10cm or 12cm (4″ or 5″) of sawdust on top of the object or objects and place the next assortment of dry clay objects on top of this layer. Fill the places in and around these with sawdust, add a further 10cm or 12cm (4″ or 5″) layer of sawdust, and so on until the whole bin is filled with alternating layers of sawdust and clay-formed objects. The top layer of sawdust, at least 10cm (4″) deep, should be level with the rim of the bin.

Light the sawdust from the top with newspaper tapers. When the top layer of sawdust smoulders evenly, replace the lid of the bin and let the fire work all the way down through the sawdust, coal and clay product filled bin. This should take twenty-four hours or more. If sudden winds increase the burning rate, use moist clay to close some of the holes punched into the rubbish bin.

After the fire has burned out in the bin, let the earthenware cool until it can be handled. Then remove the fired objects and

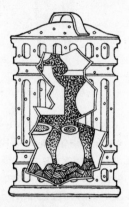

let them cool completely before further handling. They may be slightly sooty. Some of the soot will wash off and the rest will have partially glazed the clay.

Glaze-firing is impractical in such a kiln, first because there is no way to protect the wet, glaze-covered surfaces from sawdust and soot; and second because there is not enough heat generated (the heat is not even enough for successful glazing). For glaze-firing you need access to professional help and a large kiln. It is possible to get objects fired at professional potteries, art schools etc. Ask around in your neighbourhood if you do not want to go to the trouble of making a kiln.

Sculpting, carving and moulding
195 Sculpting with clay

The techniques and tools described in 174–83 and 186–93 apply. Sculpture can be coil- or slab-built (see 186 and 188) or hollowed (see 187) after it has been worked into the desired

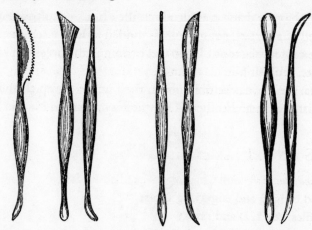

shape. Use fingers and clay-working tools to add and shape the clay. Larger sculptures should be draped over armatures (see 50–53 and 117). Hollow clay shapes, whether hollowed or worked over an armature, dry more quickly and evenly and are less likely to develop cracks and flaws than solid ones.

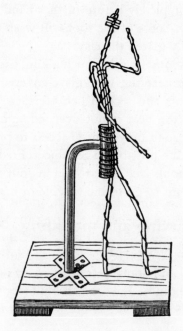

After having dried completely in the air, clay sculptures can be fired if a large enough kiln is available (see 194), or they can be cast in plaster of Paris and other materials (see 197–9).

When sculpting in clay requires more than one session, it is necessary to cover the unfinished work with a damp cloth and to moisten it periodically to keep the clay pliant and workable.

196 Soap and wax carving

Tools and materials: dull, small, long-handled knife;
pointed etching and engraving tools;
small files (see 122) and rasps;
bar of soap; beeswax; dental moulding or casting wax;
or paraffin wax; 15cm × 15cm × 2cm (6″ × 6″ × ¾″) wooden work
base; candle in holder (optional);
forged steel modelling tools

Soap, beeswax, and paraffin wax are easily carved with blunt tools. They lend themselves to being worked by children in the young age groups. Show the child how to carve and re-move slivers, incise and engrave lines and shapes, smooth or create sharp edges, and form the material to create desired shapes.

When the young craftsman has practised basic carving skills and when he can be trusted to be careful, light a candle and show him how to warm his tools for carving, cutting, whittling and shaving the material. Beeswax can be formed in the hand; candle wax or paraffin wax can be melted in a double boiler. Half-fill a large cooking pot with water. Break up candles or paraffin slabs into a second, smaller pot and place it inside the larger, water-filled pot. Bring the water to the boil until the wax liquefies. When it has cooled so that it is warm to the touch, let the child scoop it out and form it in his hand. He can carve and engrave on the wax and give it detail and texture with cold or warmed tools.

197 Making an open plaster mould

Children should be discouraged from filling prepared and manufactured moulds with clay or modelling compounds and dough (see 1–8 and 137). Materials in which papier mâché, clay, modelling compounds or plaster are cast for creative purposes, and moulds made by the child from models he has sculpted or formed, are something else entirely. There are two good reasons for making and using such moulds: to cast an object made of clay and to reproduce it in more durable material, and to make multiple duplicates of the child's creation. For example, he may wish to duplicate a modelled or incised plaque to make a necklace of identical modules.

An open mould is sufficient for any small clay object that has a flat base or back. The following steps are required to make such an open mould out of plaster of Paris for duplicating and casting models in clay.

Make sure that no undercuts exist on the original clay model as shown in the diagram. They would prevent the separation of the mould from the model once the plaster has set.

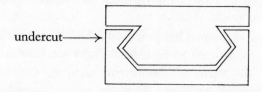

undercut———>

Place the air-dried clay model, right side up, into a cardboard or wooden box about 2·5cm (1″) wider than the model on all four sides and 2·5cm higher than the object itself. Mix enough plaster to fill the whole box. Follow the directions and proportions given in 192 for mixing plaster of Paris. As soon as it is mixed, pour the plaster slowly all around and over the object inside the box until the box is completely filled with plaster. Tap the box with a finger all around to allow any air bubbles trapped in the plaster to rise to the surface.

The plaster will set and harden in fifteen to thirty minutes. Remove the plaster cast and clay model from the box. Tap the cast to release the clay model. If it does not come free easily, attach a small piece of fresh clay to the bottom of the model and pull it gently away from the mould. The mould should now consist of a nearly perfect, reverse replica of the original. Use plaster-modelling tools to correct or smooth irregularities in the mould and to clean out any clay that may adhere. See 198 for directions on how to make clay duplicates from such a mould.

198 Casting in clay from an open plaster mould

Tools and materials: slip (see 179), mixed to the consistency of treacle; clay-modelling tools (see 186 and 195); spatula or lath, longer than the open mould is wide

Pour slip into the open mould until it is filled completely and the clay bellies up slightly. Tap the outside of the mould gently to remove air bubbles. Scrape off excess slip with the spatula or lath and level the top of the mould. After a day or two the clay will have dried enough so that it can be separated from the mould. Tap the plaster mould to release the casting. If it does not come free, press a wad of fresh clay to the casting and pull. It should then come loose from the mould without difficulty, unless there are undercuts in the mould. The mould can be used for casting additional duplicates after it has been cleaned. Any small irregularities in the casting can be corrected with modelling tools and slip. The casting can then be air-dried and eventually fired, if a kiln is available.

199 Other mould-making and casting materials

A greased plaster of Paris or rubber mould can be used for casting hollow papier mâché shapes (see 48) or ones of modelling dough. Coat an open mould or mould parts with mâché mash or modelling dough about 3mm to 6mm ($\frac{1}{8}$" to $\frac{1}{4}$") thick. Let it air-dry in the mould.

Synthetic and plastic mould-making and casting resins, including and especially epoxy, are toxic and carcinogenic. Do not allow children and young people to use these materials.

200 Mosaics

Tile- and mosaic-making are closely related. The ancient Babylonians, Egyptians, Greeks and Romans cut slabs of clay into small tiles and dried, painted and glazed them for assembly into decorative wall and floor designs and murals. True mosaics were made by cutting and breaking up coloured glass into fragments and composing complex designs and pictures with these pieces embedded in chalk mortar.

Glass mosaic tiles and plastic mosaic modules are available but children and young people should make their own materials whenever possible instead of working with pre-fabricated parts. Very young children can make paper mosaic modules (see 31); older ones can make them out of cloth snippets, leather (see 126), clay and plaster of Paris. Scrap materials such as pebbles and seeds, can also be used.

201 Clay and plaster mosaic tiles

A 3mm to 6mm ($\frac{1}{8}$" to $\frac{1}{4}$") clay slab (see 188) or plaster bat (see 192) can be incised with a dull knife and divided into small mosaic modules. Do not cut all the way through the slab or bat. Geometric and non-geometric shapes can be cut and, after the clay or plaster has dried, broken apart and sorted by shape and size (see diagram a). Shaped metal strips, metal tubes and pipes can also be used to embed shapes in plaster or clay. Or a bottle or rolling pin can be covered with strips of cardboard, wire or string, outlining a latticework of shapes (see diagram b). This can be rolled over the wet clay slab or plaster bat to incise shapes.

After the clay has dried or the plaster has set, either can be painted (see 164 and 167–9). If water-base paints are used, the colours can be made more or less waterproof if the painted

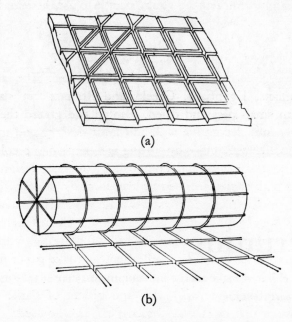

(a)

(b)

tiles are covered with several successive coatings of clear varnish or shellac (see 165), transparent glue (see 26), water glass (see 42), or acrylic medium (see 28 and 167), after the paints have dried.

Mosaic tiles can be set into chalk mortar, a sand and paste mixture, plaster of Paris or cement. Younger children will find it more convenient to work inside a cardboard box lid or wood tray whose sides are no higher than the tiles are thick. Show the child how to cover a small area with mortar or adhesive, set the tiles, and when the coated area is filled prepare the next section until the whole tray is covered with mosaic tiles.

8 Printing

Let the children make their own equipment as far as they can.
Jean-Jacques Rousseau

202 Background

If writing gave permanence to the word and allowed the events of history to become known to scholars of future generations, printing brought information within reach of all. The printed picture and word have special value in this age. The reader can re-examine what he read earlier and refresh his memory as quickly and often as he chooses. Film and TV in their present form, except for microfilm, cannot be used in this manner. Audiovisual media invite a different kind of participation from that of print (see Chapter 9) if they are to be thought-provoking and educative.

Printing as a craft can be enormously satisfying, especially for young people. It enables them to leave their mark, to experiment with combinations of forms, shapes, textures, colours and type that they can create, design and duplicate. Even pre-scholars can achieve interesting and satisfying results with a wide range of simple printing materials.

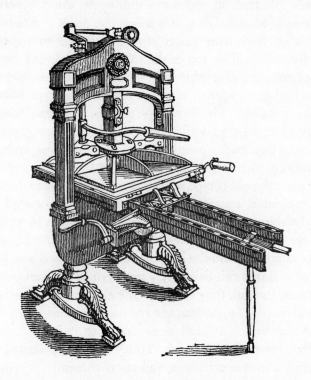

Printing was first practised in China, about AD800 – six hundred years after paper was invented there (see 13). Between AD841 and 846 the great 'stone classics' were printed in China by carving and inking stones and rubbing on paper laid over them. Twenty-two years afterwards, the first book was printed from wood blocks, and this technique for reproducing pictures and text has since developed into a fine art in China.

Printing from movable type, known to the Chinese for over six centuries, was independently invented by Johann Gutenberg in the fifteenth century in the German city of Mainz.

From Gutenberg's time to the late eighteenth century, letterpress printing remained nearly unchanged. Lithography, invented by accident in 1796, is a printing method based on the principle that oil and water don't mix. Alois Senefelder discovered, after writing a laundry list on a grease-coated stone, that its mirror image was transferred to paper inadvertently placed on top of the stone. This printing method did not compete effectively with letterpress and intaglio until photographic transfer of screened pictures and type to metal became possible. The invention of the linotype machine permitted rapid type-setting and -casting. Electrotyping, a method of duplicating printing plates for letterpress, and other innovations turned printing from a craft into an industry. More recently, phototype setting, electronic colour separation and computer controlled processes have automated and brought about a further technological revolution in printing.

These crafts, in their present-day techno-industrial forms, are far removed from the experience of children. There is just no way children can be actively involved in modern printing processes. Instead, they must practise earlier, labour-intensive methods in order to understand and use these media creatively. These techniques, though unprofitable to industry, are still required for really fine work. Today they are practised only by artists and rare craftsmen and craftswomen.

First prints
203 Blotting paper monoprints

Tools and materials: poster paints; brushes; drawing paper (see 149); sheets of blotting paper

Suggest to the child that he paints a design on the drawing paper, using brushes and very moist poster paints. Place a

sheet of blotting paper over the painting before it has a chance
to dry. Rub the blotting paper without shifting it. The
painting will transfer to the blotting paper. Place the original
and the blotted monoprint next to one another. Point out that
the monoprint is a mirror image of the original. Let the child
look at the monoprint in a mirror if one is handy. He'll
discover that the design appears there as in the original. This
recognition is important for future print-making, in which the
design cut into the block must be a mirror image of the
expected print.

204 Carbon paper duplicating

Tools and materials: bond writing or typing paper; carbon paper;
pencil or ballpoint pen

Slip one sheet of carbon paper between two sheets of bond
writing or typing paper and suggest that the child draws on
the top sheet with a pencil or ballpoint pen. By interleaving
five or six sheets of writing paper with carbon paper, he can
make several copies at a time. Point out that direct 'duplicating'
is not the same as printing, in which the original is always
reversed.

205 Potato and other vegetable prints

Tools and materials: stamp pads impregnated with stamp pad ink
or vegetable dyes, or with linoleum block water-base or oil-base
ink; bun tin filled with very thick poster colours;
brush (see 149); dull knife blade; newspaper;
potatoes; carrots; cabbage stalks; white radishes; turnips;
onions; corn cobs; any other close-fibred vegetable or stalks

Any of the vegetables, if cut in half, into sections or into
different shapes, and inked or coated with poster paint will
print. Do not encourage the child to carve a design into the

top of a halved potato. It is easier and better to carve the whole
potato half into whatever printing shape has been chosen (see
diagram).

It is best to make different shapes for each colour or to
duplicate the same shape if the child wishes to print each in

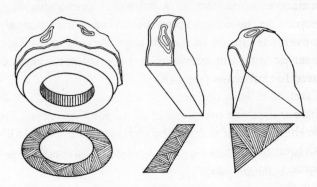

several colours. The ink is difficult to wipe off vegetable
stamps, and if the child presses one that still contains one
colour into other colours, all will soon turn muddy. The
poster colours can be painted on to the stamping surface with
a brush. Homemade stamp pads can be improvised by placing
a piece of felt in a tin lid, and coating it liberally with bottled
stamp-pad ink or vegetable dye; the ink or dye can be re-
plenished when it dries out.

206 Printing with a brayer

Tools and materials: brayer (see below);
sheet of plate glass, perspex, or plastic to roll out ink;
water-base or oil-base linoleum printing inks in red, yellow, blue,
black and white (and turpentine if oil-base inks are used);
spatula or palette knife; newspapers or other absorbent papers;
spoon; clothesline and clothespegs

A brayer is an ink roller attached to a handle. Inexpensive
brayers are made of hard rubber and are good enough for

beginners. Be sure to keep the brayer clean and hung on a nail when it is not in use. Caked printing inks ruin a brayer. Also, if left sitting on its rubber surface, the brayer will flatten and become useless.

A brayer can be used in two ways: to coat a printing block or surface with ink; and to roll over the paper that is placed on top of an inked printing block to make an impression. However, the curved surface of a soup spoon usually obtains a better printing impression than a brayer. A brayer can also be used for rubbings (see 218).

Water-base linoleum printing ink, while not as brilliant as oil-base ink, is the preferred medium for beginners. Besides, all washing up after printing can be done with water. Oil-base inks require turpentine as a solvent and cleaner.

Squeeze about 5cm (2″) of ink out of the tube on to the plastic sheet. Use a flexible knife – a spatula or palette knife – to spread the ink ribbon. Then roll the brayer over the ink, moving it back and forth until it covers a portion of the plastic or glass surface with a smooth, tacky film. If ripples and waves appear on the ink surface, it has not been spread sufficiently or it may be too thin. Let the ink dry in the air for ten to fifteen minutes and roll it out again. When the brayer is well covered with ink, roll it over the printing block. If the block has not been printed before, several coats may be needed before it is cured and the ink has penetrated the pores of the material. Move the brayer over the block from several directions. Once cured, a couple of passes with the well-inked brayer over the block, each at right angles to the other, should suffice to ink the surface for a good impression.

Once the block is inked, gently drop a sheet of absorbent paper on top of it. Do not move the paper once it is in contact with the block or it will smear. Rub the curved side of a spoon over the paper to get a good impression. The first few prints may be unsatisfactory. But these proofs let you know how much pressure to apply; whether the ink is too wet, too dry or just right; and whether the block needs heavier or lighter inking or deeper cutting in places.

Hang finished prints until they are completely dry before stacking them.

207 Scrap material prints

Tools and materials: same as 206

Any material with a deep and well-defined grain or texture can be used as a printing surface. The following is a partial listing of improvised printing surfaces.

Coarse linen or canvas cloth	Embossed wallpaper
Cardboard shapes	Bottlecaps
Plant leaves, whole or with the flesh stripped from the skeleton	Bulrushes and moss
	Pebbles
Bottle corks or shapes cut out of flat cork sheets	Sponge
	Coins
Crumpled tissue paper	Bark
Straw matting	Egg-carton tray
Raffia or string pasted to cardboard	Woodgrain and wood scraps

Ink and print any of these on to newsprint or other absorbent paper surfaces, using the techniques described in 206.

For best results with whole plant leaves, coat one side with a thin layer of paste (see 23–7). When it has dried, paint poster colour on the paste-covered surface or ink it with a brayer and print as in 206. Several such paste-covered leaves or any of the other materials suggested above, each inked with a different colour or tint, can be overprinted to form interesting designs and patterns.

Advanced printing with and without a press
208 Modular shape printing

Tools and materials: same as 205 and 206;
modular wood, cardboard, linoleum or rubber shapes

Sanded woodblock shapes, small pieces of linoleum glued to wood, dowel ends, rubber scraps and even the edges of thick cardboard strips attached to dowels or stamp handles can be printed next to and overlapping each other in one or more colours. If transparent inks are used, a third colour will appear

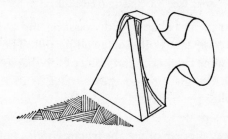

wherever two or more colours are 'trapped' by overprinting. Anyone can make printing modules him- or herself. The shapes, if they cannot be held comfortably in the hand, can be glued to a wooden board or to cardboard, provided all are the same height. Others can be attached to moulding or stamp handles (see diagram) and printed like rubber stamps. Make sure the stamp handle closely fits the shape to be printed so that the edges of the wooden base do not print accidentally along with the design (see diagram).

209 Ink engraving

Tools and materials: same as 206; sheet of heavy cardboard;
drawing paper or newspapers;
stylus or used-up ballpoint pen

Use the brayer to coat the cardboard with a thick layer of ink. Cover the cardboard with a sheet of drawing paper or newsprint and draw on to it with the stylus or ballpoint pen. Be careful not to lean on the paper, or to press a hand or finger on it. When the drawing is done, lift the paper off the ink-covered cardboard. The lines and textures engraved on the paper with the stylus will be printed on the side of the paper that rested on the ink.

210 Cylinder printing

Tools and materials: same as 206; large bottle or rolling pin; thick card; scissors (see 38); paste (see 22–8)

Cut paper strips and shapes with scissors, and paste them on the thick portion of a bottle or a rolling pin. The paper must all be of the same thickness and none of the shapes can overlap or cross. Ink the glass or perspex surface as in 206. Roll the bottle or rolling pin over the inked area, inking the raised paper surfaces pasted to it. Then roll the inked cylinder on a sheet of newspaper or other absorbent paper. The raised and inked paper design pasted to the bottle will print. With careful marking on the end of the bottle or tube where the print ends, either can be re-inked and a continous repeat pattern printed (see 214).

Similar prints can be made with twine, string, or thread pasted to the cylindrical surface, provided material of the same thickness is used in each case and none of it crosses or overlaps.

211 Linoleum block cutting

Tools and materials: unmounted battleship-grey linoleum; black India ink; or felt markers (see 143); inexpensive watercolour brush; set of linoleum cutting tools; oilstone

Unmounted linoleum is easier for young people to control while cutting. Suggest that the young craftsman designs directly on linoleum with brush and India ink or black felt marker. Explain that everything not painted black will have to be cut away and that the black-painted portions are the ones that will print.

The linoleum should be fresh, soft and not brittle. Properly instructed, children as young as five can design and cut linoleum blocks successfully. Use an oilstone to keep the cutting tools sharp at all times. The sharper they are, the less likelihood that a blade will skip out of a cut and injure the user. Instruct the child that the hand holding down the linoleum must be behind the tool at all times (see diagram on page 70). The cut should be made in a direction away from the hand holding the material. If a young person cannot be depended on to observe caution, he is too immature to work with linoleum.

Provide the child with scraps of linoleum on which to try the different cutting blades and to discover the possible variety of effects. Small cuts, dots and fine lines spaced closely or farther apart create tones and textures. The depth of the cut should be no deeper than half the thickness of the lino-leum; it should never be so deep that the fabric backing shows through. To assure a large edition of prints and that the block won't crumble, bevel each cut and never undercut the linoleum (see diagram). Point out that if the child decides to

cut letters of the alphabet or sign his name, the letters must be drawn and cut in reverse or they won't read when printed (see 203).

The block is ready for printing only after all uninked areas have been cut away. Wash the block in mild soap and warm water to remove ink and grease and then let it dry thoroughly on a flat surface.

212 Linoleum block printing in one colour

Tools and materials: same as 206;
newspaper; Japanese rice paper; or tissue paper

Ink and print the block as described in 206. Cure the linoleum
with repeated inking. Drop the newsprint or rice paper gently
on the block. Don't move the paper once it is placed or it will
smear. The first few impressions, whether printed with a
brayer or spoon or on a press, will probably be poor. Compare
each proof with the next. They will show where additional
cutting, greater or less pressure, or more or less ink may be
needed to make the best possible print.

After printing, wash the block with solvent (turpentine, if
oil-base inks were used; water, if water-base inks were used)
and then in mild soap and warm water. Clean ink off brayer
and glass or perspex plate and hang up brayer and prints (see
206). If quite a lot of ink is left on the glass plate, the ink can
be scraped off with a spatula and wrapped in plastic for future
use.

A properly cared-for block is good for many editions and
prints.

213 Linoleum block printing in more than one colour

Tools and materials: same as 211 and 212;
sheets or roll of wax paper

A two-colour print – red and black, for example – requires that
two blocks be designed, cut, and printed, one for each colour
(see 220). Design and print the black plate as in 212. Pull
several good proofs. Then wash, dry, and apply a heavy
coating of orange ink to the same block and print it on a sheet
of wax paper. Place the printed wax paper sheet upside down
on a second, uncut linoleum block the same size as the first.

Rub the back of the wax paper to transfer the design to the second linoleum block. Peel off the wax paper. Let the ink dry thoroughly on the second block if the impression is a good one. If the print is poor, wash the ink off the block and try again, as before.

This transfer of the design from the first block to the second is essential so that the second colour cut can be registered more or less exactly with the first. Precise registration is difficult without a printing press, but you can come close. Once the orange ink is dry on the second, uncut block, paint in whatever areas you have chosen to print in the second (red) colour with black ink or felt marker. Be sure to 'trap' (overlap) colour areas that are supposed to meet and have adjoining edges. Paint the black ink about 3mm ($\frac{1}{8}''$) over the orange ink in these places. Then cut away all but the black-painted areas.

Pull a number of proofs of the second block until it is cured. Then ink the block with the chosen second colour and lay one of the black proofs on the second block. If both linoleum blocks and the paper are cut to exactly the same size, registration will not be too difficult. Print the second colour and check the proof for any additional cutting or inking that may be needed. Then print a whole edition of the red, second block.

In printing, the lightest colour is always printed first and the black last. After the red edition has been printed and has dried, ink the black block again. Place one of the red prints as squarely as possible on the black block, face down, and print. A fairly high percentage of the prints will be sufficiently well registered to be considered good if reasonable care is exercised in printing.

A third, fourth, or more colours can be cut and printed in the same way. Each requires its own block; transfer of the other colours to wax paper and then to the next block that is to be cut; painting in of the desired colour area; cutting and printing, as before.

Close registration is possible only on a press on which corner stops can be attached so that, once a block is positioned, the paper can be registered and laid in exactly the same place for each colour. Such paper stops can be taped to a linoleum block cut much larger than the picture that is to be cut and printed, even when no press is available.

Another way to make colour prints is to cut and print the black block and hand-stamp it with modular shapes, each inked with different colours (see 208).

214 Repeat-pattern making and printing

Tools and materials: same as 205–13

Potato, vegetable, scrap materials, cardboard, clay, slab, plaster and cylinders, as well as linoleum blocks, can be designed to repeat themselves in all directions. Repeat patterns can be used for fabric and decorative paper printing. The simpler the design, the easier it is to repeat it so that the top and each side of one print fit other sides of the same design, when printed adjacent to each other. Cylinder printing assures a continuous repeat design in one direction, though the ends of the cylinder must be designed carefully so that prints match edge to edge.

215 Fabric printing

Tools and materials: same as 214; rawhide mallet;
white or plain coloured cotton or silk

Because of the size of the material required even for a scarf, fabric is usually printed with repeat patterns (see 214). All the detailed techniques apply. Oil-base printing inks or fabric colours, available from art and craft material suppliers, are used to print on fabrics that, when thoroughly dried after printing, are to be washable.

Cover a large table with thick layers of newspaper. Keep the unprinted fabric rolled up at one end. Unroll enough of the fabric to cover the table and tape it to the table edges so that it is slightly stretched and wrinkle free. Place the inked block, face down, on the fabric, starting at one corner of the cut end.

Beat the block with the mallet for a good impression. Re-ink the block and make a second impression next to the first one, and so on until the whole fabric surface, taped to the table, is printed.

Stretch several lengths of twine across the room beyond the far end of the table and drape the printed fabric over it (see diagram). Tape the next length of fabric to the table and

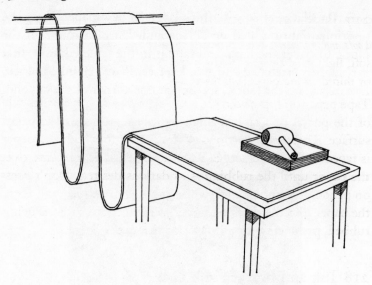

continue printing as before. Cease printing when you run out of drying space. After the printed fabric has dried it can be rolled up and the printing process continued as before.

216 Rubbings

Historically, as pointed out in 202, rubbings from stone preceded the invention of printing. Finding surfaces from which interesting rubbings can be made is a worthwhile quest. It can help make children and young people aware of their surroundings. The following are common surfaces that lend themselves to rubbings, in addition to those listed in 207:

Coins; pebbled and cut glass; plastic or wire mesh;
vegetable grater; brick and cement blocks;
weathered wooden boards; metal manhole covers; tombstones;
stone, metal, or plastic plaques and reliefs

217 Pencil and graphite stick rubbings

Tools and materials: No 6B pencil or graphite stick;
soft, lightweight paper: tissue paper; rice paper;
or thin drawing paper; masking tape

Tape paper on top of the object to be rubbed. Use the flat side
of the pencil or graphite stick to rub gently over the paper
surface. The raised portions of the design to which the paper
is taped will soon emerge. Rub more pencil or graphite over
the paper until the rubbing is as dark as desired. Don't press
on pencil or graphite stick while rubbing. Pressure will force
the paper into the recessed portions of the object that is being
rubbed, producing a muddy print that lacks detail.

218 Ink and brayer rubbings

Tools and materials: same as 206; masking tape

Ink the object to be rubbed with the brayer, gently lay the
paper on the inked surface, and tape it. Print with spoon or
clean brayer as in 206. Valuable objects, wood, clay or stone
carvings should never be inked directly since it may not be
possible to clean them perfectly. To rub them, use the technique described in 217.

219 Stencil printing

Stencil printing has value only if the child makes his or her
own stencils; prepared stencils may seem like an amusing
pastime but undermine a child's creative drive (see 1–7 and
137).

220 Scissors-cut stencil printing

Tools and materials: brown wrapping paper; waxpaper;
or wrapping paper soaked in vegetable oil; scissors (see 38);
masking tape; drawing paper or card (for printing);
poster colours (see 149); large, stiff stipple brush

Paper folding and cutting techniques (see 32–41) can be
applied to stencil cutting with scissors. Very young children
can create interesting and unique stencils that they can print
in one or more colours.

After the child has cut the design of the stencil, tape one
edge to the drawing paper or card on which it is to be printed.

Mix the poster colours to a stiff paste. Provide only one colour
of the child's choice as a start. Others can be added later. Then
show him or her how to dip the tip of the stipple brush into
the colour, deep enough to cover only the end of the bristles.
Apply the paint around the edges of the cut-out portions of the
stencil with a rapid up and down motion of the brush. The
brush will require frequent dipping in the paint. After the
edges have been given a coat of colour, work the brush
towards the centre of each opening in the stencil, until all

are coloured. There is no need to cover the whole paper with a thick layer of paint. A stippled, light coating will give the print texture.

Do not remove the stencil from the paper until the paint has dried completely. Then unfasten the tape and lift off the stencil, and the design will be revealed underneath. If the paint crawls under the stencil edges it means the paint mixture was too watery. Two (or more) colour stencils can be designed in the same way as multicolour linoleum blocks (see illustration).

Various colour effects and designs can be created by printing the same stencil a second time, turned to a different position on the paper after the first printing, and using a different colour for a subsequent impression. Different stencils can be printed in sequence, one after the other, each in different colours or tones, but only when the preceding coat of paint has dried. Care must be exercised when stencilling one poster colour over another. Do not press hard on the stipple brush or the preceding layer of paint may be moistened and dissolved.

Repeat-patterns on paper and fabric (see 214 and 215) can be printed with stencils. Once each impression has dried, move the stencil to the next position and print.

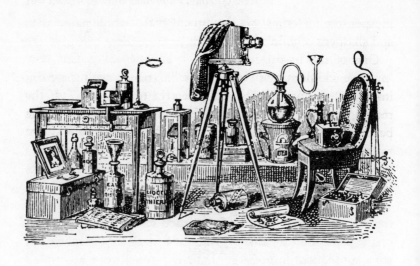

9 Photography, films and sound recording

Choosing is creating. *Friedrich Wilhelm Nietzsche*

221 Background

TV sets, still- and motion-picture cameras and projectors, TV and sound tape equipment are now found in nearly every school and in most homes. Yet few young people know how to use any of these media creatively. Nineteenth-century craft and activity books for children invariably explained how to make a pinhole camera, blueprints of leaves and flowers, and flip-book and zoetrope animations. Recently developed photographic and sound-recording processes and techniques offer even more stimulating challenges to young people who know how to use them. Creative work in these media involves inexpensive materials and equipment that is readily available, and sharpens a child's judgement.

One of the by-products of such experiences is that they 'provide children with critical skills for becoming active, intelligent, appreciative and selective consumers of the moving image'.* With the proliferation of audiovisual media beamed at children at home, in the classroom and at the

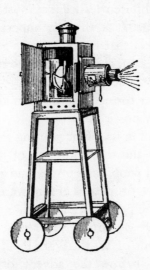

cinema, and the amount of time today's child spends just watching and listening to them, he or she had best learn to become selective and critical or he or she will be swamped by them. Active involvement in these techniques allows children to become participants where now they are too often spectators.

This chapter describes how media can be used in a variety of ways and on many levels as means of expression. Children need little equipment and much stimulation if they are to use them inventively. They need guided experiences that allow them to acquire background and skills; that lead them to-

* Lewis Mumford, *Art and Technics*, New York: Columbia University Press, 1952

wards a craft approach in using the materials and making discriminating choices of what they wish to state and how to state it. Used for these purposes rather than as instant magic, the media can be excellent learning tools. The child, who is impatient by nature, receives the rewarding results of his or her creations almost at once. But do not allow this instant quality of the materials to be the sole source of satisfaction.

Few of today's children realize that most of these processes are of recent vintage. It is virtually impossible for a modern child to comprehend that his parents or grandparents knew a time without TV, for example. And with rapid technological change, new processes descend on us before we have explored, used, understood or formed any opinion about the potential of those we already possess.

Photography, still in its infancy during the latter half of the nineteenth century and the beginning of this one, was used primarily to portray people and places, and to imitate painting. The unique, creative properties of film were not realized until the 1920s, when the possibilities of still- and motion-picture film were explored by artists and early filmmakers. The propaganda demands of World War II and the popularity of picture magazines before the advent of TV caused the flourishing of documentary still photography and the picture story, now largely a thing of the past. The Polaroid camera and Land's new colour process, among other instant picture-taking features of today's still- and motion-picture equipment, enable anyone to snap a picture or to immortalize baby's first steps.

The instant quality of many of these processes tends to foster the delusion that the mere possession of the equipment and its casual use enable anyone to be creative. It's not so. According to records kept by processors of amateur film, the repertoire of what is photographed is extremely limited and deadly dull. And most tape recorders are used primarily for business, professional and surveillance purposes and to lift radio and TV shows or records. This chapter is intended to help young people make better use of the technologies, to be creative producers rather than passive consumers.

222 Photography without a camera

A camera is not needed to take pictures. A variety of photographic papers and easily available and quite harmless chemicals exist that make many photographic experiences possible for young children at little expense. The processes are simple; the greatest emphasis can be placed on originality and invention, looking for and discovering materials and subjects for image-making, and arranging them in new and surprising ways. Once the initial technique of picture-taking and print-making are mastered, suggest to the child that he or she experiments with exposures of negatives and prints and discovers variations on conventional techniques.

223 Lenses, prisms and kaleidoscopes

Plastic and glass lenses and mirrors that enlarge, reduce and invert images; prisms that break up light; and a kaleidoscope that creates optical repeat-pattern illusions in motion can be stimulating and diverting toys for children. They also teach. A hair or a leaf seen through a magnifying glass opens up a new world to which the child might otherwise remain blind. The changing patterns of form, colour, texture and light, created by paperclips, glass fragments, snippets of paper, or grains of sand seen through a kaleidoscope, awaken the child to patterns, motion and visual surprise. It's no coincidence that David Brewster, the inventor of the kaleidoscope, should also have given birth to the stereoscope in 1844, by which two pictures of the same scene, each viewed from a slightly different angle through a stereopticon, create a three-dimensional illusion. The stereoscope became a favourite Victorian amusement for children and adults and is still used to help children discover the startling world of optics. All these are essential preparations for an interest in and an understanding of what we know today as 'the media' – photography, film, animation, sound and videotape, and holography.

224 Shadow pictures

Tools and materials: cut paper shapes;
darkened room and a single, strong light source: lamp, candle or
flashlight

Shadows thrown on the wall in the shape of faces, animals and
other figures made entirely with the fingers of two hands have
long amused small children. The wiggling ears of the shadow
rabbit were children's movies and TV, long before the
invention of the latter. Shapes cut from black paper can add to
the illusion of moving shadow pictures (see diagram).

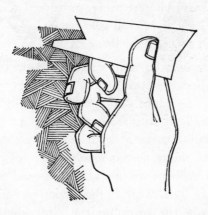

Appreciating and eventually imitating the creation of shadow
and silhouette shapes and how they can be combined and
projected helps children learn to see and compose images.
These are essential disciplines in photography and especially
in making photograms (see 227).

225 Photocollage

Tools and materials: black and white and colour photographs cut
from magazines and travel folders; card; scissors (see 38);
paste (see 21–8)

Encourage the child to cut out photographs and parts of
photographs and paste them next to, over, and partially under

each other on card to make decorative pictures or to tell a story. A photograph of a standing man can be pasted upside down so that he stands on his head.

226 Blueprints

Tools and materials: blueprint paper; dilute peroxide;
sheet of plate glass or perspex; large sheet of heavy cardboard;
two enamel, rubber or plastic trays, larger than the cut sheets of blueprint paper to be used;
two sheets of heavy blotting paper; or clothesline and clothespegs (to dry prints); pitcher of clear cold water;
scrap materials; choose those that have well-defined silhouettes

Design and arrange the scrap materials on the blueprint paper sandwiched between cardboard and glass plate. Follow directions on the paper package label for light source and exposure time. Wait until the exposed paper turns light blue. Then remove objects and glass plate and soak the paper in the tray filled with dilute peroxide solution until the unexposed portions turn brilliant white and the exposed portions of the paper turn dark blue. Wash in the second tray filled with clear water and hang the print on the clothesline or place it between two sheets of blotting paper to dry. Double-exposures are not possible.

227 Direct photograms

Tools and materials: package of No 2 photographic contact paper;
paper developer (either powder or in solution); hypo;
fresh water;
three enamel, rubber or plastic trays, each larger than the photographic paper size; red darkroom safety light;
100-watt lightbulb and shade;
two-socket overhead light fixture with separate switch for each socket; large sheet of heavy cardboard;
sheet of plate glass or perspex;

rubber or plastic apron (to protect against chemicals); rags; scrap materials; choose those that have well-defined silhouettes

Here a wide range of grey tones, as well as sharp black and whites, and multiple-exposures are possible. Start by letting the child print silhouettes of his or her own hands.

It is important that the child learns to remove the photographic paper from the package one sheet at a time only, when the red safety light is switched on and the 100-watt bulb is switched off, using the two-socket fixture. Make sure he closes the paper package carefully so that the paper is not light-struck later. Place the paper, emulsion (shiny) side up, on the cardboard and arrange scrap materials on it. Cover both with perspex. Mix all chemicals in advance, each in its own tray, according to the instructions given on the package labels.

Arrange the package of photographic paper to the right of the actual exposure surface and the three trays to the left – developer tray first, hypo tray next, and clear water tray last, in that order. The cardboard and glass exposure surface should be directly under the light source. Switch on the 100-watt light bulb only during the exposure period. Keep the red safety light switched on during development and fixing of the print.

Teach the child to count: 'One thousand and one, one thousand and two . . .' for controlled timing of each exposure. On completion of the exposure time, switch off the white light and switch on the red safety light. Remove the glass covering and objects from the paper and dip the paper face down in the developer. Agitate the print, grasping it by one corner and moving it rapidly back and forth. Keep the paper fully immersed in developer. Turn it over for inspection once in a while. When the image comes up, leave the paper face side up in the developer until it reaches the desired intensity of tone. Then let the developer run off the paper as it is lifted out of the tray and immerse the print in the hypo tray to fix the image. Follow the timing directions on the paper and hypo package labels. Agitate as before. On completion of the fixative bath, let the hypo run off the paper and immerse the print in clear water. The longer the print washes in clear water, the less likely it is to stain in time. Dry the print between sheets of blotting paper. Weight the blotting paper to keep the print from curling.

The developer is good for many prints as long as the image comes up on the exposed paper with sufficient intensity of tone. However, each print will need longer time in the developer, which weakens with use. Change the hypo after each dozen or so prints and the water after each three or four.

After several prints have been made, suggest that the child tries to make a double exposure. Arrange the objects on the paper as before, but expose them for only half the previous time. Then rearrange the objects on the paper for a second exposure a little shorter than the first. When developed, fixed and washed, the print, if properly exposed, will contain overlapping images in tones of grey as well as in black and white. Encourage the child to play with double-, triple-, and multi-exposures of silhouettes for different designs, effects and gradations of tones.

228 Slide-making

Tools and materials: slide projector;
slide binders (available in photographic supply shops);
clear acetate or plastic film cut to size;
black and white (and coloured) acetate inks and solvent;
inexpensive brush; drawing pens and holder;
transparent, coloured, pressure-adhesive acetate

Let the child draw and paint on the clear acetate or design with snippets of pressure adhesive, transparent coloured acetate, or a combination of both. Each completed slide can be inserted in a slide binder and projected. A light show can be given with a series of these prepared slides.

229 Cameras

In making photograms the child learns the relationship between negative and positive image making. The child becomes involved in printing and development, in preparing handmade negatives and processing them. All that remains to be learned is the optical photo-negative making and developing process, for which a camera is essential. It is important that the child plays with these materials as much as with his perceptions. This is why a pinhole camera is a useful first camera.

230 The pinhole camera

The first camera – before the invention of photosensitive materials – the camera obscura, was used by artists to project and reduce real-life scenes on a screen for copying. The pinhole camera is its direct descendant. As shown, it projects the image on to photosensitive film or paper to produce a negative which, after it has been developed, can be printed like the photograms in 227.

How to build a pinhole camera:

Tools and materials: same as 227;
matte black poster board; or cardboard 6·25cm ($2\frac{1}{2}''$) square;
sheet of aluminium foil; No 10 sewing needle; black card;
sharp knife blade; triangle and T-square;
black poster paint, or blackboard paint and solvent (to paint cardboard if no black poster board is available);
small, inexpensive paint brush;
100mm × 125mm ($4'' \times 5''$) film or photographic paper (see below for details)

Read 61, 62 and 66 for details on how to design, cut, score and build the 11·25cm × 13·75cm × 12·5cm ($4\frac{1}{2}'' \times 5\frac{1}{2}'' \times 5''$) box shown in diagram (a). Cut out the square in the front of the box

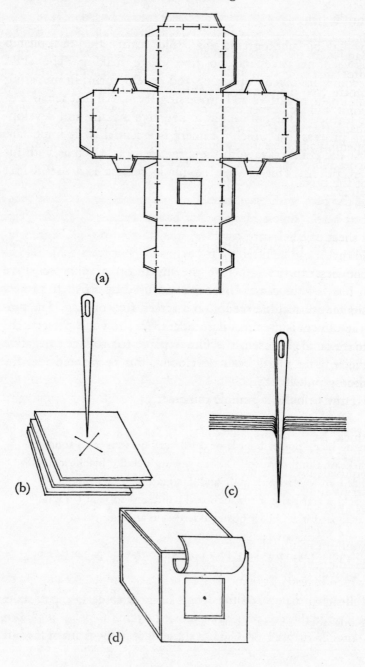

(a)

(b)

(c)

(d)

for the 'lens'. Cut out two pieces of poster board or cardboard and a piece of foil, $6\cdot25$cm $\times$ $6\cdot25$cm ($2\frac{1}{2}'' \times 2\frac{1}{2}''$) square. Sandwich the foil between the boards and tape the edges, after marking diagonals on one of the boards to find the centre (see diagram b). Push the needle through the centre point, but no deeper than about halfway from the point to the shank (see diagram c). Centre the foil on the inside of the lens opening and tape it down firmly. Now fold the box along the scored lines and lock or paste all tabs except those on the back of the box. Tape all exterior edges, except those on the back of the box, with black tape. Paint the inside and outside of the box black (unless black poster board was used). Finally, tape a sheet of black card over the lens, as shown (see diagram d), so that it can be lifted up for exposure, but stays folded down between exposures.

For paper negatives: Use Kodabromide paper F.1 or F.2 or a similar substitute available in 100mm $\times$ 125mm ($4'' \times 5''$) size. Tape the paper, emulsion (shiny) side facing the lens opening to the inside back flap of the camera in a dark room, using only the red safety light as illumination. Close the back flap and, if necessary, tape the edges. Make sure that the camera lens flap is tightly closed and take the camera into sunlight for exposure.

For film negatives: Use Kodak Royal Pan Film 4141, extra thick base, or its equivalent in 100mm $\times$ 125mm ($4'' \times 5''$) sheet size. Or a roll of 120 or 620 Kodak Tri-X Pan Film or its equivalent can be cut, in a dark room, into $7\cdot5$cm- ($3''$-) long strips and taped on the back flap of the camera – one at a time, as above.

To expose the film: Place the camera on a firm base with the sunlight behind it. The required exposure is too long for hand holding. It's a good idea to tape the camera to the surface on which it rests. To expose the film, raise the lens cover for the following exposure times:

Kodabromide Paper	bright sun:	cloudy bright:
F.1 or F.2	2 mins;	8 mins

| Tri-X or Royal Pan Film | bright sun: 1–2 secs; | cloudy bright: 4–8 secs |

Film processing: Use Kodak Tri-chem pack and follow the instructions on the package, or whichever chemicals are recommended for any other film that is used.

Printing the negative: Follow the directions given in 227, except that the paper negative is placed emulsion (shiny) side up on the bottom and the photographic paper on which it is to be printed, emulsion side down on top of it. Hold the sheets together in close contact with the perspex plate. Experiment with exposures, starting with fifteen seconds. For film negatives, place the photographic paper on the bottom, emulsion side up and the film negative directly on top of it. Start with a ten-second exposure. Develop the print as directed in 227.

Obviously a pinhole camera is a crude instrument; yet remarkably good photographs can be taken with it. Double-exposures can be made, although this requires a good deal of experimentation with exposure times, negative development, and printing. The benefit of the camera lies precisely in that. The young photographer learns by trial and error and gets the feel of the material far better than with an instant camera.

231 The low-cost camera

Any number of very low-cost cameras are available, excellent for children and young people. It is much wiser to economize on equipment and be lavish with film than vice versa. Tripods, exposure meters, flash and strobe units, fancy camera bags and the host of gadgets that are the supposed essentials of photography just get in the way of learning how to use camera and film. Today's high-speed films make flash equipment virtually unnecessary, and the rest is useful only to the most advanced amateur or professional and for special purposes.

232 Hints on picture taking

Photography is a creative medium only if the child is highly selective about what he shoots, chooses the portion of subject or scene that is most significant, and the precise moment of the peak of action. Get the child used to looking through the viewfinder, scanning the scene, object, or person, and deciding which segment is most significant and representative of the whole. Suggest that he moves closer or farther away, to shoot from a selected angle at eye level, from above or below, and at different exposures. Suggest to the child that he photographs the puddle instead of the whole street, the leaf instead of the forest.

Most cameras include two lens controls: the 'f' stop and the shutter speed control. The 'f' stop determines how large a shutter opening is to be used; and the shutter speed control determines how long the shutter remains open when the picture is taken. Before placing film in the camera, open the back of the camera and let the child look through the lens at all the 'f' stops. He'll be able to see how the shutter opening is enlarged or reduced with each change of 'f' stop.

Explain that as the shutter opening is reduced, the overall sharpness of the picture, from background to foreground, increases. When the shutter opening is enlarged the foreground remains sharp, but the background becomes increasingly fuzzy. The photographer can control emphasis by using the different 'f' stops. For example, by stopping down the shutter opening as far as it will go, given the proper lighting conditions, the overall effect will be that of a picture postcard in which everything is sharp and there is little distinction between foreground and background. But this is not how the human eye sees; it focuses on what is most important at the moment and blurs the rest. To photograph a closeup, the shutter should be open as wide as possible. The fore-

208 Photography, films and sound recording

ground should be in sharp focus if the camera is properly focused. The background will be blurred, as it is in real life when you look close at something.

The 'f' stops must also be related to shutter speed. The speed with which the shutter opens and closes determines how much light strikes the film. This is why fast shutter speed settings are used on sunny days, but slower speeds are required on cloudy days or indoors. The illumination determines which 'f' stop can be used, since it increases or reduces the amount of light that enters the camera.

Suggest to the child that he follows the 'f' stop and shutter speed directions printed on the instruction sheet inside each film package for different lighting conditions, for his first exposures of the film. Then, for the next shot, reduce the shutter speed by one setting and increase the 'f' stop by one setting. Keep changing the exposures for the same photograph for several successive shots, take notes, and compare the results when the roll of film has been developed and printed. This is how a young photographer learns to control his medium.

Film speed (the light sensitivity of the emulsion on the film) is another control factor. Today's fast films make flash and strobe units unnecessary for all except extremely bad lighting conditions and special or professional camera work. Also, by mixing controlled amounts of borax with developer, fast film speeds can be increased even more and film exposed under extremely poor lighting conditions can produce interesting, readable pictures. Finally, by careful printing and paper development, portions of a negative can be 'held back' and others emphasized.

The beginner must learn how to hold a camera. If he wiggles even slightly at the moment of exposure, the picture will be blurred. A tripod is unnecessary for all exposures of a half second or less. Let the child press the camera against his chest while his finger is on the trigger. Then, just before he presses the trigger, let him hold his breath until the picture is taken. This assures relative immobility.

A negative can be cropped (only a portion selected) for printing. But the ability to select, compose and photograph exactly what is wanted with the camera, rather than in the enlarger, is the essence of the photographer's art.

233 Film development

Tools and materials: development tank for the film size used; film developer and hypo; stop bath; red safety light; sink and running water; sponge-tipped squeegee tweezers; thermometer; funnel; clothesline and clothespegs; weighted clips

Follow the directions in the film package about which developer to use. Follow the directions provided with developer and hypo for mixing the chemicals, and for the temperatures at which they should be used. Unroll the film in total darkness or by red safety light and strip away the paper backing. Thread the film on the wire holder of the development tank, then replace and close it again. If the development tank includes a light trap, the rest of the work can be done in daylight.

Pour the developer into the tank through the funnel. Cover the tank opening and let the film develop for the time stated on the chemical package. Shake the tank periodically during the development time. At its end, pour the developer into a brown bottle and store it in the dark for future use. Keep in mind that film developer, like paper developer (see 227), weakens with use and that future development with the same batch of chemicals will require more time. Pour stop bath and hypo into the tank for the required amounts of time. Stop bath halts development; hypo fixes the image on the film. These chemicals can also be re-used two or three times if they are stored where it is cool and dark. After the hypo has been emptied from the tank, let clear water run into it and, after an initial rinse, open the tank and stand it under a running tap for twenty minutes.

When the film is thoroughly rinsed, remove the wire holder from the tank and, grasping the clear leader of the film, unwind it. Run the sponge-tipped squeegee the length of the film from top to bottom to remove excess moisture. Do not repeat this operation or it may streak the film. Hang the film by its clear leader from two clothespegs attached to the line. Attach a weighted clip to the bottom edge of the film and make sure that it does not touch any surface or object while drying. Leave it hanging undisturbed until completely dry. While removing weighted clip and clothespegs, and whenever inspecting film hold the negative by the edges and never touch the surfaces of the negatives. Fingerprints tend to become embedded in the emulsion and they show up in the finished prints.

234 Contact printing

Tools and materials: same as 227;
200mm × 250mm (8″ × 10″) photographic contact printing paper; magnifying glass; scaleograph; red grease pencil

Whether you send exposed film to a commercial processor to be developed, or whether you develop it yourself, it pays to contact-print film before ordering or making enlargements.

Never cut the roll of film into individual negatives. Cut it into strips of a length that enables them to fit, lengthwise, on a sheet of 200mm × 250mm (8″ × 10″) paper.

Contact-print the negative strips as in 227. After the contact sheet is dry, examine each print with a magnifying glass and check off the ones that are worth enlarging. Each picture can be cropped (a selected portion marked) with a scaleograph (see diagram), available from photographic supply shops.

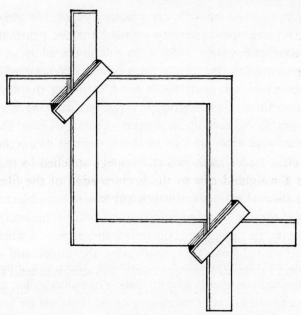

Mark the cropped area with a red grease pencil to decide which portion of each negative should be enlarged.

235 Enlarging

Tools and materials: same as 227;
photographic enlarger with interchangeable film carriage for different film sizes

Photographic enlargers are expensive. Unless one is owned or a dark room equipped with an enlarger is available, the chosen negatives must be sent to a processing laboratory for enlargement. One can be found through the Yellow Pages of the telephone directory. Provide the processor with a marked and cropped contact sheet (see 234) and the desired enlargement size.

If an enlarger is available, place the selected negative in the carrier, leaving the rest of the filmstrip protruding on either side. Switch off the regular white light and switch on the red safety light. Place an ordinary piece of paper, the same size as the photographic paper to be used for the print, on the easel under the enlarger. Move the enlarger head up or down and focus until the portion or the whole of the negative that is to be enlarged is in sharp focus and fills the paper area. Then place one sheet of photographic paper (see 227) on the easel, emulsion (shiny) side up, and print as in 227. Different print densities, gradations of tone, and other effects can be created when printing with an enlarger. Several prints may be required before the best combination of exposure and development time is discovered for a given negative.

236 Colour photography

Tools and materials: any camera; colour film (check size, number of exposures, film speed; whether indoor or outdoor film; and whether colour prints or transparencies are furnished on development)

Colour film cannot be developed by children or in a makeshift or home dark room. Colour film that can be developed and printed by amateurs is now available, but it requires a fully equipped dark room. Most colour film needs to be sent to commercial processors for development. When buying colour film ascertain whether the processed film is returned as transparencies (slides) or as colour negatives and prints. The colour fidelity of transparencies is always better than that of negatives and prints, if the exposure was correct, but they require a projector for viewing. Colour prints can be made from transparencies, but good type C or dye transfer prints are prohibitively expensive. They are used only for commercial reproductions.

Any camera can accommodate colour film, but note that the exposure times required for colour film are very different from those for black and white. Be guided by the exposure directions provided for different lighting conditions in the directions packaged with the film. For best results bracket the exposures by shooting at one more 'f' stop and one shorter exposure, and then at one less 'f' stop and one longer exposure, for each scene, in addition to the combination suggested in the instructions.

The best outdoor results in colour photography are obtained in the early morning or late afternoon, or at any time on slightly overcast, dull or foggy days: in other words, not in brilliant sunshine. Photographs taken under bright, ideal black and white conditions tend to be too highly coloured and to look artificial even when exposures are perfect. For good indoor colour, strobe or flash bulbs 'bounced' off the ceiling or wall are required, unless high-speed film and very long exposures with a camera set on a tripod are used. Once the basic techniques are mastered, suggest to the young photographer that he tries unorthodox effects – shooting into the sun at very fast exposures, or extremely long exposures at night.

237 Animation and movie-making

In a parallel to still photography, a child doesn't need a movie camera to make movies. It is much more interesting for him if he starts making movies without a camera and without film, using only materials to hand. In the following movie-making projects and animations, the use of tape recorders (see 242–7) is implicit to add dimension to the art, wherever possible.

238 Thaumatrope

Tools and materials: 10cm to 15cm (4″ to 6″) white card discs; large sewing needle or hole punch (see 18); thread or twine; wax crayons (see 140); or cut-out photographs, coloured paper and paste (see 24–8)

The thaumatrope was probably the first movie invention. Punch two holes on opposite sides of each disc and thread a loop of thread or twine through each set of holes. Draw or paste two related but different pictures, or paste two such photographs, on each side of the disc. For example, place a bird on one side and a birdcage on the other. Now wind up

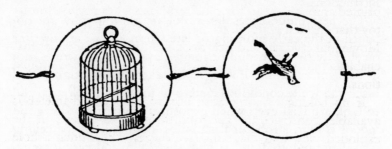

the string by holding each loop in two fingers of each hand and swing the disc in an arc in one direction until it is thoroughly twisted. Then pull at each end in an opposite direction, relaxing the pull as the string unwinds and the disc begins to twirl. The bird will appear to be inside the cage. If the string is pulled and relaxed alternately, the illusion will continue indefinitely. Primitive as this toy may be, it illustrates the stroboscopic effect on which all motion-picture production is based.

239 Zoetrope

Tools and materials: 25cm (10″) diameter × 5cm (2″)-high round cheese box or baking tin; or cardboard constructed turntable (see diagram c); four or more 35cm × 13cm (14″ × 5¼″) strips of white card; or paper pasted together to this length and width; one 35cm × 13cm (14″ × 5¼″) strip of black card; or black paper pasted to this length and width; burnisher; compass; ruler; right-angle triangle; HB pencil; scissors; sharp knife blades and holder (see 69); masking tape; paperclips; crayons; poster paint and brush (see 149); coloured paper and paste (see 24–8); coat-hanger wire and pliers;

two 2·5cm (1″)-diameter washers with a 3mm ($\frac{1}{8}$″) hole in each;
blackboard paint and brush; paint solvent;
heavy cardboard work surface

The nineteenth century's zoetrope came complete with printed animations. In the nineteen-fifties I designed a similar toy that enabled children to make their own animations – the Movie Maker. The following are plans for a movie maker that enables children to create drawn, painted and pasted animations.

If no baking tin or cheese box of the right diameter is available, construct the zoetrope turntable as shown in the exploded view and diagrams (see diagram c). Punch a hole in the centre of the cheese box, baking tin, or constructed turntable with the hammer and nail. Add the handle as shown and brush two coats of blackboard paint on the outside of the turntable.

Fold one of the 35cm × 13cm (14″ × 5$\frac{1}{4}$″) white paper strips in half; halve twice more. Crease the folds sharply with the burnisher and cut slots on both sides of the folded sheet as shown (see diagram a). When unfolded, use this sheet as the template (see diagram d; and 65) for the other black and white paper strips. Mark the slots on them and cut them out with a sharp knife blade. Place the paper on a thick sheet of cardboard for cutting so that the tabletop is not damaged.

(a)

(b)

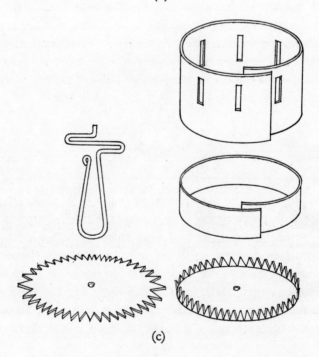

(c)

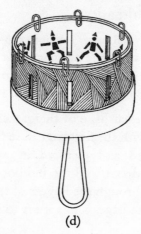

(d)

Paste the black slotted paper strip to the inside rim of the turntable (see diagram c).

After slots have been cut, draw animations between the slots of the white card strips. On completion of each sequence, insert the white strip in the turntable, lining up slots cut into the black and white papers. Attach the white paper strip to the black with paperclips all round (see diagram d). Spin the turntable while looking through one of the slots. The pictures will appear to move.

240 Flip book animation

Tools and materials: several paper signatures, 8–16 pages each, folded and gathered. Use bond or lightweight drawing paper. Each page need be no larger than 5cm × 7·5cm (2″ × 3″); hole punch; paper-fasteners; wax crayons (see 140)

Draw a picture on each page of the gathered signatures in a sequence, starting with the first page. Use the same animation techniques described and pictured in 239. When all the pictures have been drawn and the flip book is filled, run the edges of the pages through the fingers of the other hand. The images drawn on the pages will appear to be in motion.

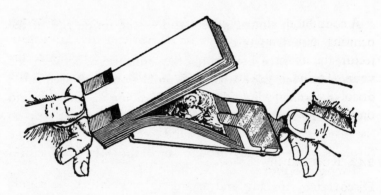

241 Drawing and scratching on film

Tools and materials: 8mm or 16mm movie projector; 720 frames of clear 8mm or 16mm film leader; acetate inks in different colours; solvent; student grade watercolour brush; drawing pen nibs and holder; needle point, or tipped etching tool

Movie film runs through camera and projector at the rate of twenty-four frames per second; 720 frames of clear leader will produce a thirty-second film, which is about as much as a young film-maker can handle without becoming tangled up.

If pre-striped, single-sprocketed clear leader can be obtained, the film-maker, in addition to drawing his animation on film, can scratch sound on to the sound track (see 244).

A continuous animation on film can be created by drawing, painting and scratching on film. When run through a projector, the image will appear to be in motion. Suggest to the young film-maker that he lets the design flow together and dissolve over the whole length of the film, rather than drawing on individual frames (see diagram).

242 Recording

Discovering, making and arranging sounds can be highly creative experiences, which call imagination and selective judgement into play, heightening the capacity to listen, to distinguish the meaning of sounds, and to use them inventively. Try turning off the sound on your TV set, letting children guess what sounds go with the pictures unfolding before them, or make up the dialogue.

The skills required for operating a cassette tape recorder are slight. All that needs to be learned is the buttons to push for record, playback, fast forward and reverse winding of the tape, how to insert and remove the cassette and how to clean the sound head. Transferring sound from one recorder to another is only slightly more complicated.

243 Sound instruments

One of the problems that stands in the way of a creative use of sound is that this subject is studied only in elementary science classes. Classroom experiments with sound usually don't concern themselves with meaning and sequence. The human voice is a remarkable solo instrument, able to imitate a wide range of sounds and effects. Encourage the child to mimic animal noises, the sounds of cars, sirens, bells, trains, aeroplanes and boat whistles, water rushing in torrents or rain drops splattering. Scrap materials can aid in such sound production: sticks rubbed or struck on wood; a fingernail scratched over fabric, glass, or eggshell; a dowel or metal spoon struck or rubbed over a cooking pot lid. These are common experiences that enable a child to experiment with sounds.

Homemade musical instruments can be constructed that introduce the child to rhythm and interval. Rubber bands stretched across a box (see diagram a), or a series of water glasses, each filled to a different level (see diagram b) and

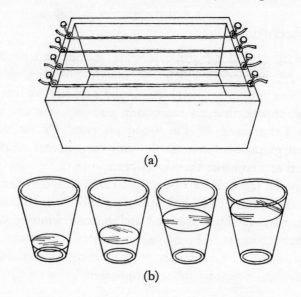

(a)

(b)

struck with a dowel, can produce musical sounds and be recorded on tape. As the child plays back sounds he has created, he'll get ideas for producing others.

244 Scratching sound on film

Tools and materials: 720 frames of pre-striped, single-sprocketed clear leader (8mm or 16mm);
8mm or 16mm sound film projector;
needle point, or tipped etching tool

Given the basic understanding that sound is recorded on magnetic tape in wave form, a child can make a spontaneous sound track on film. Scratch on the opaque coloured band on the unperforated edge of the film with the needle or etching tool. By varying the configuration of the scratches (see diagram), a variety of high, low, screeching and bleeping sounds

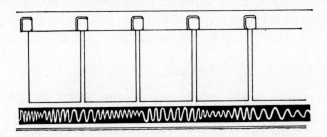

can be created that are made audible when the film is run through the projector. If such a sound track is to accompany a directly drawn animation on film (see 241), it is important to keep in mind that the sound head in the projector 'reads' the sound track twenty-six frames beyond the picture it matches. In other words, the picture projected on frame No 1 is accompanied by the sound on the track next to frame No 26.

245 Finding sounds

Encourage the child to take his tape recorder with him wherever he goes – to the zoo, airport, circus or fun fair, and on any excursion to places where unusual or interesting sounds are likely to be found. At home he or she can record the miaowing of the cat, the barking of the dog, the ring of the telephone, or the kettle boiling on the stove. These sounds, recorded on tape, can be built into a library of natural sound effects (see 246) that the child can use in his or her play and in making animations or movies.

Demonstrate how the meaning of sounds changes when they are rearranged in different sequences:

Cat's miaow	Cat's miaow	Footsteps	Footsteps	Door slam	Door slam
Footsteps	Door slam	Cat's miaow	Door slam	Footsteps	Cat's miaow
Door slam	Footsteps	Door slam	Cat's miaow	Cat's miaow	Footsteps

These, or any other three sounds, can be arranged in six different ways, each sequence conveying a different set of events and meanings.

246 Making sound effects

Professional movie makers and TV producers do not rely exclusively on natural sounds recorded on location; for example, thunder is produced by shaking a large metal sheet; rain, with metal foil or by pouring dried lentils or peas on a wood or metal tray. Inventing sound effects and recording them on a tape recorder is a useful experience. These effects can be edited into story-telling tapes (see 247) or used for animation and film-making.

247 Story-telling on tape

Suggest to children and young people that they tell or read stories into the tape recorder, producing and using sound effects (see 243–6) at appropriate moments to dramatize the story. When the tape is played back, let the child listen and make suggestions for future improvement, slower speech or reading, greater separation of words, better pacing and pronunciation.

10 Fibre craft

If between the ages of five and fifteen, we could give all our
children a training of the senses through the constructive shaping
of materials – if we could accustom their hands and eyes, indeed
all their instruments of sensation, to a creative communion with
sounds and colours, textures and consistencies, a communion
with nature in all its substantial variety, then we need not fear
the fate of those children in a wholly mechanized world.
Bernard Shaw

248 Background

The first likely products of weaving – wind breaks, fences and
palisades – were probably inspired by man's awakening to a
consciousness of animal behaviour – nest building and spider
web and cocoon spinning. This probably led to imitation and
the eventual discovery of original weaves and patterns. These
skills were inevitably applied to various purposes and products – hair ornamentation, baskets, fish traps (still used in
Malta), coracles (wattle-daubed wicker boats), ritual offering

vessels, chests, huts, and even chariot, carriage and wagon bodies. Between the period of the rude beginnings of this craft and its eventual, partial replacement by work in other materials, twisting, spinning, weaving and knotting vegetable fibres became possible as man's ability to make tools – bone awls, threaders and needles – developed.

Many examples of woven baskets, and of course cloth, are pictured in Assyrian and Babylonian murals, sculptures and reliefs, and in later Egyptian and Greek friezes and vase decorations. The common use of wicker baskets is reflected in the story of the infant Moses, left in a basket on the shore of the Nile. Basket-making and its products were frequently considered holy and associated with religious sacrificial rites. During the time of the Roman occupation of Britain, Druids are reported to have woven huge replicas of the human figure, filled with votive offerings, which were burned to the ground during annual religious ceremonies. The bearskin caps of the Guards are lined with wicker even today.

A way had to be found to lengthen and strengthen softer fibres. Flax, jute, sheep's wool, cotton and, in China, the excretion of the silk worm, needed to be twisted into continuous strands to provide fibres for weaves that eventually replaced animal skins as man's clothing. By the time of the flowering of the Incan and Egyptian empires, weaving had become so refined that the closeness and delicacy of the cloth has been seldom matched since.

Primitive weaving was very slow. The warp threads (the vertical strands; see 262) had to be lifted one by one so that the weft (the horizontal strands; see 262) could be passed over and under them alternately to form the weave. The invention of heddles by an unknown genius of the distant past allowed each set of warp strands to be lifted alternately as a group, as shown in the previous illustration; and the shuttle, which holds the weft strand, as shown below, to be thrown rapidly. It is essential to understand these simple principles of weaving,

the proper terms, and the basic mechanism so that they become second nature to the young craftsman. The need to speed up the weaving process made invention and improvement of equipment a matter of concern, second only to agriculture, to those who first experimented with mechanics and water power. This mechanization undermined the consumer's reverence for the product and the labourer's reverence for his work. The latter declined to machine-minding.

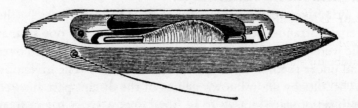

Until some of the basic braids, weaves, and knots are mastered, it is impossible to be inventive. Encourage children to invent their own designs even if they re-invent many that were traditional in the past. Conventional weaves can be readily deduced from the basic ones. Should any child or young person need to know these for practical reasons, he or she can find the particulars in the existing literature.* What is far more important and of primary concern is that the child learns to create and recognize patterns as

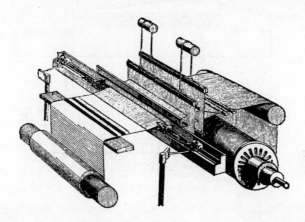

a result of his experience inspired by this and the following chapter. For these reasons some of the less creative aspects of the craft, like caning, have been deliberately excluded. Caning is mostly limited to particular patterns by utility and necessity rather than convention, and the emphasis here as elsewhere in this book is on developmental learning.

Winding and stringing
249 Unravelling

Tools and materials: old wool sweater or other garment; cardboard shuttle (see diagram a)

Unravelling a discarded garment and winding the wool into a ball or on a shuttle can be an interesting activity for nursery and kindergarten age children. The garment should be made of thick, coarse fibre, preferably wool. The turned-over warp

* G. H. Oelsner, *A Handbook of Weaves*: Dover Publications Inc, 1952

strands (see 248), or bound-off knitting (see 270), should be cut through with scissors at the hem so that the child can separate the weft easily (see diagram b). Caution him not to

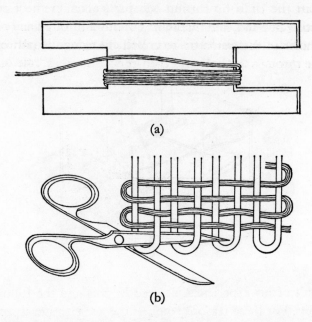

(a)

(b)

unravel more wool than what he can wind on the shuttle at one time. The wool thus unravelled can be used in many of the projects described above and below. (See also 17–20, 29, 30, 89, 127, 158, 183 and 207.)

250 Cord construction

Tools and materials: open cardboard box; cardboard or wooden frame; hole punch (see 126 for round drive punch and mallet), or hand drill and bit (see 93); ball of twine, yarn or wool

Punch holes in the sides and bottom of the cardboard box or construct an open framework of any desired shape and drill holes into all frame members (see diagram a). The constructions shown are representative examples only. The idea is not to thread the twine through every hole but to choose those that, when threaded, make the design interesting.

Start the child by cutting off about 30cm (12″) of twine, knotting one end, and threading the other through any one of the holes in the frame or box. Pull the whole length of the twine through the hole and then choose another hole on any

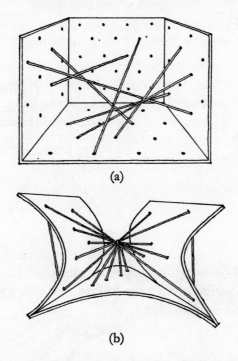

(a)

(b)

opposite side through which to thread it. Pull the twine tight and continue weaving across the box or frame from hole to hole. Whenever the length is used up, knot more twine to its end until the design is finished. Different-coloured yarn can be knotted together for multicoloured effects.

More experienced young people can combine warp (vertical) designs with weft (horizontal) designs, weaving over and/ or under to create almost any configuration that grows spontaneously out of the work. Caution the child not to pull too hard on the weft strands, or he may distort the cardboard box sides or frame. If the frame is very solidly constructed, it is possible to distort the warp design deliberately by tightening up on the weft strands (see diagram b).

251 Pasting

Tools and materials: string, twine, wool, thread and fibres; paste (see 21–8); sheet of heavy cardboard or card

String, twine, wool, thread and fibres can be dipped in paste and used as collage materials (see 29); or the cardboard can be given a thick coating of white or acrylic paste and strands laid into it in patterns and combinations of the child's choice. (See also 30, 89, 125 and 183.)

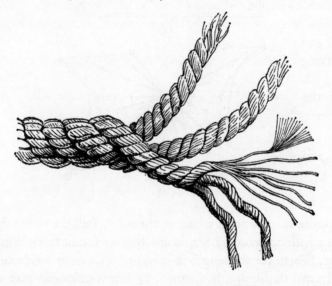

252 Twisting, braiding and knotting

Knots are part of not only the weaver's craft, but the sailor's. There are more than 150 different ways of knotting and splicing twine and rope, but only a small number of them are of practical value to the young craftsman. The first ropes were probably made of twisted vines, thong or animal gut. The knot was an inevitable invention born of the need to keep long hair from interfering with full movement, to secure bundles, and to tie off ends of coarse braids and wicker weaves. The Greek Gordius supposedly tied a knot in 3,000BC, whose ends were so cleverly concealed that no one could discover how to untie it. Legend had it that whoever untied the Gordian knot was to rule the entire Asian continent. According to myth, Alexander the Great severed it with a stroke of his sword and fulfilled the prophecy. Folklore and superstition surround the knot all over the world. The knot has been a part of rituals from tying the umbilicus of the new-born to the marriage ceremony.

A child can be shown how to make his own rope. Take a bundle of single or twisted fibres – twine, string or thread – and gather it evenly at one end. Tape the end securely with masking tape and secure in a vice or G clamp (see 90 and 91). The whole bundle of fibres should be about 6mm ($\frac{1}{4}''$) thick. Cut the other end even and insert it in the chuck of an ordinary hand drill. Turn the drill and a rope will begin to

form (see diagram). It's a good idea to moisten the fibres before twisting and then dry them while still held under tension by vice and drill. Bind the end near the drill chuck with tape before unfastening the rope.

When a child has learned how to tie shoelaces, he is ready for some of the projects described below. Each braid and knot, by itself and in combination with bead work and weaving patterns, can produce individual and inventive results. As with all other craft, don't try to teach too much too soon.

253 Cat's cradle

It is appropriate to mention here this Eskimo and Oriental game, Cat's cradle, played with a loop of string of which the ends are tied together and stretched between the outstretched palms of two hands (see diagram). It develops finger dexterity

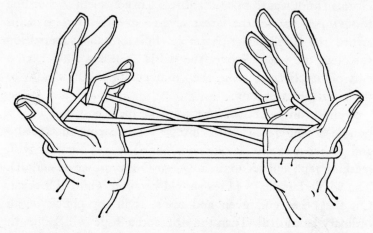

and an understanding of some of the properties of fibres. A child can weave intricate designs of his or her own invention in endless variation, using the basic principle of cat's cradle.

254 Braiding

Tools and materials: cane; rushes; maize husks; grasses; reeds; raffia; hemp; willow twigs; wheat, rye, or oat straw; fern stems; honeysuckle vine; wool yarn; twine or string (see below); scissors

Each fibre used in braiding, as in basketry, caning and weaving, requires special preparation. The following describes the methods appropriate for each material:

Straw: Gather at harvest time. Cut off sheaf with scissors. Select only those straws of which the thin (top) end can be inserted easily into the thicker tubular bottom end to make longer straws if required. Soak straw in water overnight before plaiting or weaving.

Grasses (sedge or slough grass is best): Gather during summer

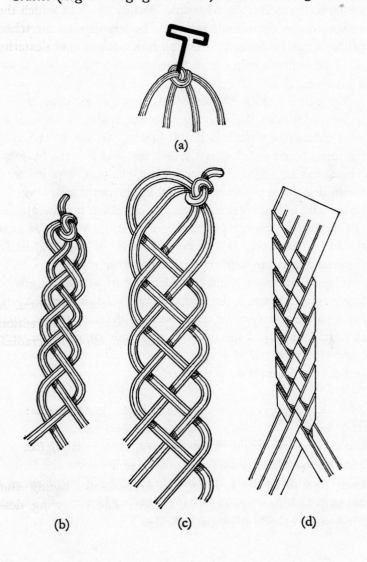

(a)

(b)   (c)   (d)

and autumn. Cut near ground with scissors. Cut off tips and remove outer covering. Dry indoors in the shade. Use dry, but dampen slightly after braiding or weaving and then press between blotting paper and cardboard on which weights are placed evenly.

Willow and rushes: Gather before the end of summer. Clip off tips and dry indoors in the shade. Rushes can be used whole, or split down the middle followed by scraping off the sticky pitch on the inside surface with a knife. Soak in cold water for fifteen minutes before use and keep wrapped in a damp towel until used.

The various braids shown in diagrams b–d are in ascending order of difficulty, each involving more strands. Whenever an even number of strands is braided (four, six, and so on), fold the fibres so that each end is a different length and additional strands can be added at different places. Cross two or more of the folded fibres at the creases and secure the folded end to a board with a T pin (see diagram a). Except for hollow grasses and straws, which can be fitted end to end, overlap the next strand by about 5cm (2″) when an addition is required. Braid the strand into the work rather than knotting it.

When a sufficient number of lengths or a long length of fibre has been braided, the fibres can be coiled and formed into flat or hollow shapes, or coiled around different forms, such as bottles, boxes, balloons and slab-built or other pottery (see 188). Such coiled shapes can be either tied or sewn together (see diagram d on page 259).

255 Knotting

Tools and materials: twine or string

The ten most basic knots and how to splice rope are shown below (see diagrams a–l). One or a combination of several can be used in macramé (see 256), weaving (see 257–65), bead work (see 265) and braiding (see 254).

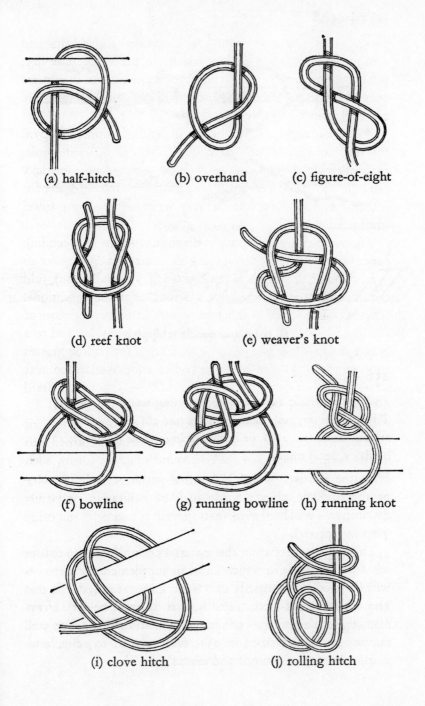

(a) half-hitch   (b) overhand   (c) figure-of-eight

(d) reef knot   (e) weaver's knot

(f) bowline   (g) running bowline   (h) running knot

(i) clove hitch   (j) rolling hitch

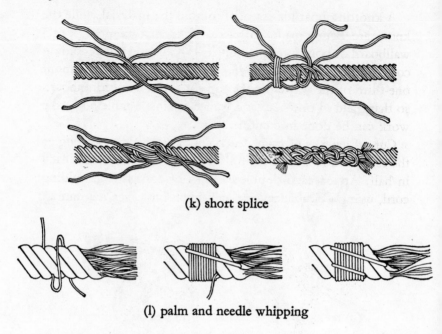

(k) short splice

(l) palm and needle whipping

256 Macramé

Tools and materials: twine or jute; knotting board (see below);
T pins; scissors; embroidery needles (see 268);
crochet hook (see 269); or leather lacing needle (see 127);
beads or metal rings

Macramé consists of tightly knotted patterns made of twine
or thread. The objects made may be utilitarian or purely
decorative – wall hangings, mats, jewellery and belts and other
wearing apparel.

The steps in preparing the material are uniform, no matter
what will be made or which knots or supplementary materials
will be used. Customarily two basic knots are used, the reef
knot and the half-hitch (see 255, and diagram below). However, these, singly or in combination with each other as well
as with those described in 255, can be used to achieve an
infinite variety of designs and effects.

A knotting board is essential to hold the material while the knots are being made. A piece of 20cm × 30cm (8″ × 12″) wallboard or polystyrene is sufficient. Knot and pin a 'holding cord' to the board. The holding cord should be pinned about one-third of the way from the top edge of the knotting board so that, held in one's lap and leaned against a table edge, the work can be done in comfort.

Cut off lengths of twine, each about eight times as long as the estimated length of the finished product, and double each in half. Attach each doubled length of cord to the holding cord, using a double reverse half-hitch knot (see diagram a).

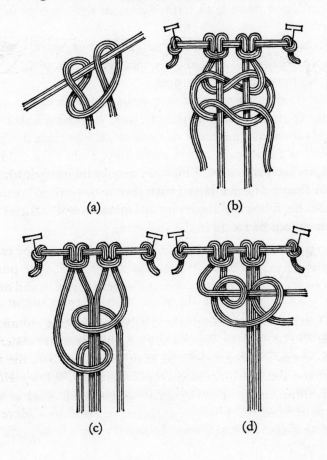

(a)   (b)

(c)   (d)

(The width of the finished work depends on the number of double strands knotted to the holding cord.) Begin knotting, using one or another of the standard macramé knots shown above (see diagrams b–d); but bear in mind that any others can be improvised or combined with those shown (see 255).

It is important to keep the holding cord taut and to add T pins to secure finished portions of the work as close as can be to the cord ends not yet knotted. The finished work should be securely pinned to the holding board. If the work becomes uncomfortable because it is too close to the bottom of the board, unpin the knotted, finished portions and the holding cord, and move both farther towards the top edge of the board.

Beads, rings, and other ornamental findings can be knotted into the work or to its ends or edges as it progresses, depending on the craftsman's purpose.

For children in younger age groups or less experienced young craftsmen, the lengths of twine and the numbers of strands should be kept to a minimum. Two or three doubled lengths of twine, each a foot or so long, tied to the holding cord, suffice for a start. Emphasis should be on spontaneity rather than on formal repeat patterns: no pre-printed pattern should be followed. Examples of more complex forms of macramé can be found in the literature.*

257 Weaving

The weaving process is the same whether spun or natural fibres are used. Weaving as a whole, not by product or material, is discussed below. Once a child has mastered the basic skills, he or she can apply them to any material or purpose. The reader is urged to read 248 and to explain the basic warp and weft principle to the child before introducing him or her to these crafts.

* Mary Walker Phillips. *Macramé*, London: Pan Craft Books, 1972

258 Interweaving

Tools and materials: paper or leather strips (see 20, 42–6, 127 and 128; and diagrams below); or fibres (see 254); or twine, wool yarn or thread; sheet of heavy cardboard; heddle sticks (see 262); scissors; masking tape

A sheet of paper or split leather, cut into strips but not all the way through, and taped by the uncut edge to the cardboard (see diagram a), becomes the warp. An identical sheet or strip, cut but not fully separated into strips and laid alongside the warp at right angles, becomes the weft. The weave can be angled (see diagram b).

Fibres and yarn can be used similarly, the top ends of the warp and the ends on one side of the weft being taped together, after the fibres are laid down side by side (see diagram c).

The advantage of this type of interweaving is that it bridges

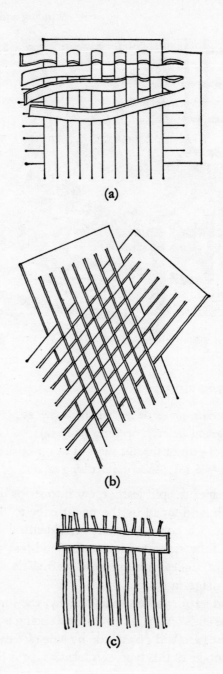

(a)

(b)

(c)

the gap in skills between braiding and weaving. Warp and weft strands are easily arranged and kept in order. If the number of warp and weft strands is kept to seven or nine each, any pre-school nursery or kindergarten child can learn to weave in this manner.

259 Paper weaving
See 42–6.

260 Wicker work and basketry
(See also 254.)

A comparison of the various weaves used in fabrics and in wicker work shows that there is very little difference in the working methods required for weaving natural fibres like rushes, reeds and palm fronds, and spun fibres like wool,

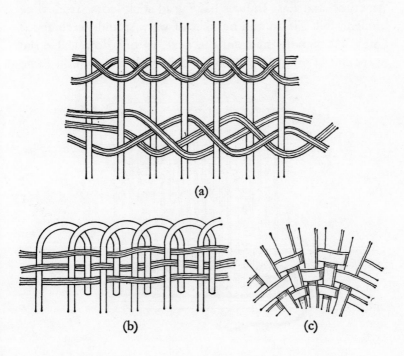

(a)

(b)   (c)

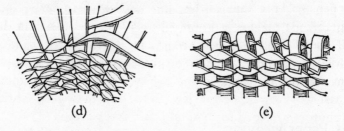

(d)   (e)

cotton and silk. Broad-leaf fibres can be slotted, bent or crossed to form variations in the warp, or the weft can be twisted (see diagrams a–e). Except for these differences, the same basic working methods apply to natural and spun fibres.

261 Stick loom

Tools and materials: wool yarns; thread; or fibres (see 258 and 260); two dowels; heddle sticks (see 262); shuttle; scissors

American and East Indians have used stick looms from time immemorial. Tie an odd number of warp strands, each about 6mm ($\frac{1}{4}''$) equidistant from the next, to one dowel. Tie the other end of each warp strand to the other dowel in the same

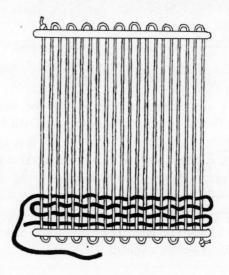

manner, so that the dowels are parallel when hung (see diagram). Suspend one dowel overhead or from a nail in the wall. Insert the heddle sticks as in 262. If yarn or thread is to be used as the weft, wind it on a shuttle and begin the weave from the top, working down. Use the heddle stick to force the last woven weft strand close to the already woven fabric. No shuttle is needed for natural fibres and grasses.

If a shuttle is used, pass it alternately from left to right and from right to left. Do not distort the weave by pulling the warp strands together. When the warp is filled and the weave is completed, withdraw the dowels and heddle stick, tie the end of the weft to the last warp strand, and tie adjacent warp strands to each other, using any knot that serves the purpose (see 255) or seems decorative.

When fibres, grasses, or wicker are woven in this manner, the warp and weft strand ends are either turned over (see diagrams b and e on pp. 241–2) and secured in the weave, or they are sewn together (see 254, 268 and 276).

262 Frame loom

Tools and materials: wood or cardboard frame (see diagram a);
wool yarn, string or fibres (see 258 and 260);
heddle stick (see diagrams b and c); shuttle; scissors

Though a frame loom is customarily used only for heavy rug weaving, it is especially useful to young people for all kinds of weaving that are adapted especially for the purpose. The wood or cardboard frame can be any size. Drill holes in the top and bottom of the frame, 6mm ($\frac{1}{4}$") or less apart. Leave enough room at the sides (see diagram a) so that the yarn or fibre can be woven. String the warp and tie it top and bottom. Insert the heddle stick (see diagram b). Turn the heddle stick to lift alternate sets of warp threads. Towards the end of the weave it will have to be withdrawn and the remainder woven without it. Weave with a shuttle or threader.

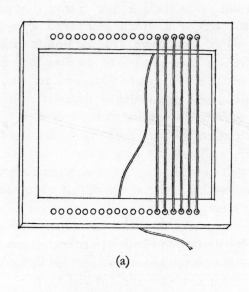

(a)

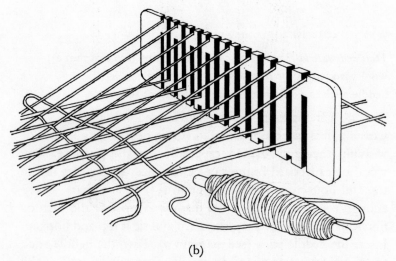

(b)

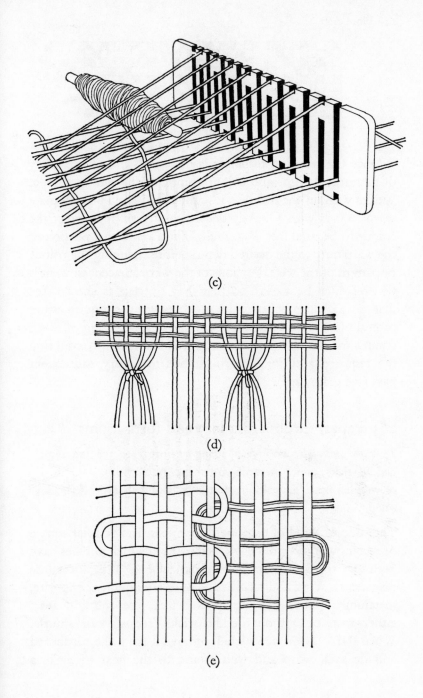

(c)

(d)

(e)

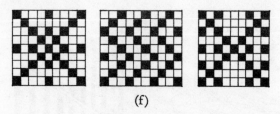

(f)

Once the weaving principle is understood, a great variety of patterns, designs and colour combinations can be woven. Weave without the heddle stick. Bind any section of alternate warp strands with a loosely tied piece of yarn or twine of the colour to be used (see diagram d). Then weave that portion of the warp only to the desired depth before changing the colour or pattern of the weft. Portions of the warp adjacent to what is tied off must be woven so that they overlap as shown (see diagram e). Diagonal or more complex weaves require either careful planning on graph paper in advance or tying off warp strands for the first pass of the shuttle and carefully counting the required additional warp strands for every subsequent pass (see diagram f).

263 Paper, cardboard and wood form looms

Tools and materials: wool yarn, string or fibres (see 258 and 260); heddle sticks; paper or cardboard shapes (see 67–72); or wooden base (see below); shuttle; scissors; sharp knife blade; ruler

The simplest kind of cardboard loom consists of a flat square or rectangular piece of heavy cardboard in which notches have been cut, top and bottom, at about 6mm ($\frac{1}{4}$″) distances (see diagram a). Wind and secure each warp strand under opposite, matching notches and weave as before (see 260 and 261), either with or without heddle sticks (see 262) or shuttle. When the weave is completed, remove it from the cardboard and tie each warp and weft strand to the next to make a

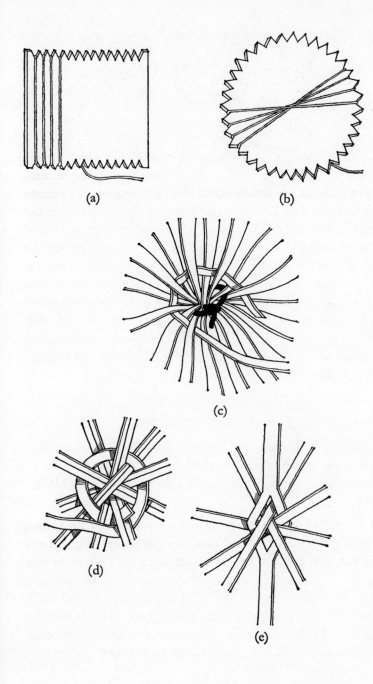

(a)

(b)

(c)

(d)

(e)

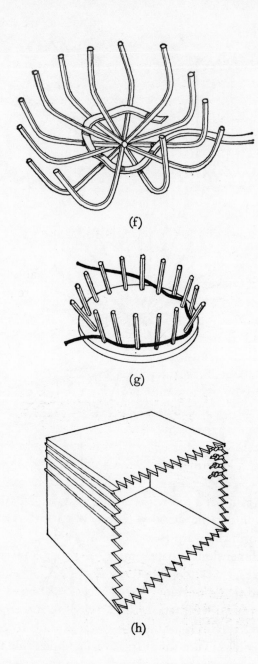

(f)

(g)

(h)

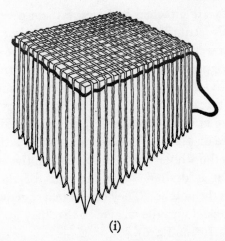

(i)

fringe or, if wicker is used, tuck warp and weft ends under the
first and second rows of the weave (see 260). Fibre weaves can
also be hemmed or sewn at the edges (see 254, 268 and 276).

A round piece of cardboard can be similarly notched
around its edge and the warp threads secured and strung as
described above. Start the weft at the centre, weaving around
and around, over and under, working towards the outer edge
(see diagram b). Flat natural fibres (see 254) do not require
such a template for round, flat or hollow woven shapes. They
can be notched and crossed (see diagrams c–e) and, if required,
the ends can be turned up to form the warp (see diagram f).
Permanent wooden bases with holes drilled around their
edges are also used for wicker work trays and baskets. Pass
the fibres under the wooden base and up through opposite
holes to form the warp (see diagram g).

Open dimensional shapes made of paper and cardboard,
tubes, boxes, tin cans and bottles can be used as templates for
wicker and fabric weaving. Cut notches, drill holes or secure
the warp thread with tape on two opposite top edges of the
shape (see diagram h). Attach the weft strands to one of the
remaining sides. Turn the shape over, its open side facing the
table. Now stretch the weft strands across the side to the edge

of which they are attached and weave them over and under the previously strung warp strands on the bottom surface only. As each weft strand completes its weave, tie it to the top edge of the opposite side of the shape (see diagram i). Turn the shape right side up when the bottom has been fully woven. Using a new thread or fibre, tie one end to the very edge of the bottom weave at one corner, and start weaving all round the four sides (see diagram i). This method can be adapted to any shape. When the whole weave is completed, the template can be withdrawn if desired, after the ends of the fibres are released from the notches. They can be tied together, hemmed or sewn or tucked into the weave, so that they do not unravel (see 254, 261, 268 and 276).

264 Weaves

Tools and materials: same as 258–63

Whole volumes are dedicated to the wicker and fabric weaves that have been invented through the ages.*† As far as children and young people are concerned, the emphasis should be on experimentation, improvisation and invention, once the basic processes are understood. The warp can consist of multi-coloured strands or strands strung in a sequence of colours or a variety of fibres. The weft need not be woven over and under each warp strand. Two or more warp strands can be woven in regular or irregular patterns. Different-coloured yarns or fibres can be interwoven in regular or irregular sequences (see 261). Or different-coloured weft strands can be joined end to end for random patterns.

The drawings (see diagrams a–d) show some of the conventional weave patterns. These are not to be copied; instead they can suggest how weaves, braids, knots and skills can be

* Navajo School of Indian Basketry, *Indian Basket Weaving*: Dover Publications Inc, 1971

† G. H. Oelsner, *A Handbook of Weaves*: Dover Publications Inc, 1952

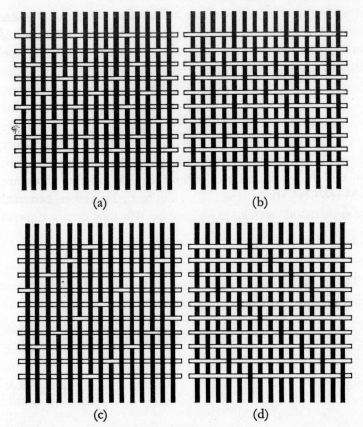

(a) (b)

(c) (d)

combined, enabling a child to improvise his or her own fabric or wicker patterns.

265 Bead weaving and stringing

Tools and materials: beads (see 181);
string and twine; or threader (see 17)

Pre-schoolers enjoy stringing beads, macaroni, and drinking-straw ends. (See also 17.) This develops finger dexterity and the discovery of patterns. More advanced bead work is usually done on a loom,* but for most purposes the bead

* Mary White, *How to Do Bead Work*: Dover Publications Inc, 1972

stringing method shown here suffices (see diagram). In combination with braids, knotting and macramé (see 254, 255 and 256), they permit invention of an infinite variety of bead stringing designs.

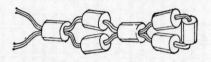

Needlework
266 Canvas work

Tools and materials: plastic mesh; punch needle (see diagram a); coloured wool yarn

Choose the wool after purchasing the mesh. It is important that the yarn is heavy enough so that it cannot slip out of the mesh easily, once stitched to it. This method of stitching, also possible with a simple threader attached to the yarn end, can be used to design and make multicoloured pile fabrics.

Thread the punch needle for the child or attach the threader (see 17, or diagram a). Show him or her how to pass the yarn through the mesh, the slotted side of the punch needle facing as shown, leaving as long a yarn loop on the underside of the mesh as the desired length of pile. Show how to feed yarn through the needle and hold the loop on the underside to assure that successive loops are more or less the same length. Different-coloured yarns, threaded into the punch needle and sewn into the mesh at various intervals, can allow the young craftsman to create colourful designs.

After the mesh is covered with stitching, turn it over and cut through the top of the yarn loops as shown (see diagram b). For permanence, cut a sheet of lightweight cardboard, canvas or linen that matches the size of the stitched mesh

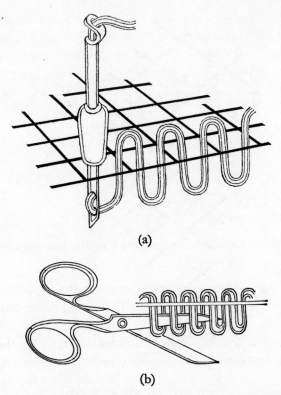

(a)

(b)

exactly, cover it with a coating of fabric glue, and paste it to the underside of the mesh before cutting the loops.

267 Knotted hook stitching

Tools and materials: latch hook (see diagram a); coarse plastic mesh; coloured wool yarn

This technique also produces a pile (see 266). Make a loop of yarn and slide the latch hook over it (see diagram a). Pull the hook down over the loop but leave it large enough so that more yarn can be fed through the loop later. Bring the hook holding the yarn loop down through one of the mesh openings, feeding the loop into the next adjacent mesh opening

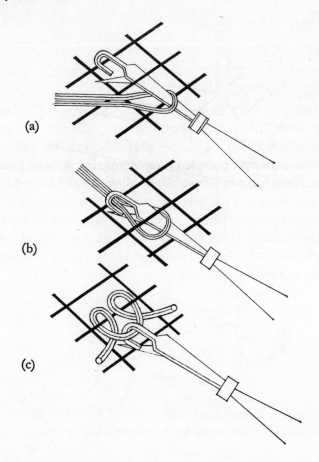

(a)

(b)

(c)

(see diagram b). Pull the free double strand of yarn through the yarn loop to form a double half-hitch (see 255, and diagram c). Cut the doubled yarn ends evenly to form the pile. If a number of different colour yarns are used, designs and pictures can be woven in this manner.

268 Embroidery

Tools and materials: tapestry or lacing needle (see 127);
coarse woven linen or canvas; yarn or heavy coloured thread;
embroidery frame; or heavy cardboard frame

Embroidery is closer to sewing than to weaving. It is related
to both and serves as a good first introduction to basic
stitches which, singly or in combination, allow the child to
be inventive and yet complete simple projects without losing
interest. Keep first projects small and allow the child to explore
the possibilities of each stitch shown to him by using it in
spontaneous sewing. Stretch, tack or staple the linen or canvas
to an embroidery frame, available in needlework shops, or a
simple frame made of heavy cardboard. The basic embroidery
stitches are shown below (diagrams a–k and 276).

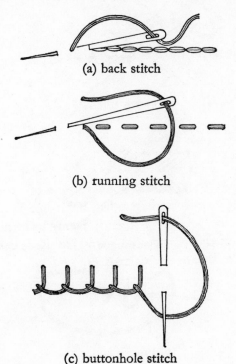

(a) back stitch

(b) running stitch

(c) buttonhole stitch

(d) chain stitch

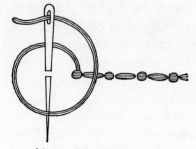

(e) coral knot stitch

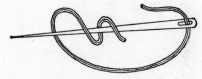

(f) stem stitch

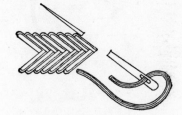

(g) fishbone

(h) French knot

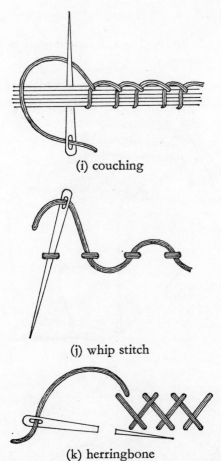

(i) couching

(j) whip stitch

(k) herringbone

Many of these stitches can be 'whipped' and bound with a thread of another colour (see diagram i).

Fine embroidery is usually done on densely woven fabrics; the coarser weaves allow the child to make evenly spaced stitches, using a tapestry or lacing needle without being confused. He can count intervening mesh spaces if he wishes. In couching, two or more threads are laid parallel on the fabric and then sewn on the material, using any of the basic stitches.

269 Crochet

Tools and materials: crochet hook; coloured wool yarn;
wool box (see diagram a)

The ball of wool should be kept in a cardboard wool box in
which a hole has been punched and the end pulled through

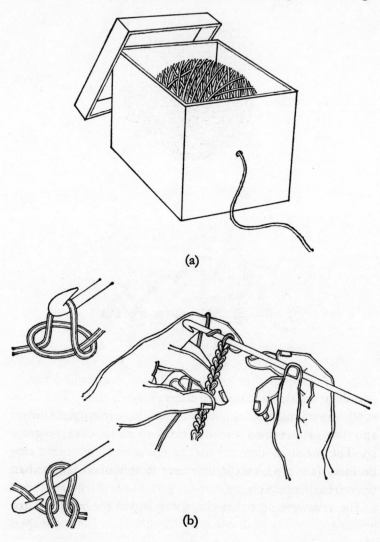

(a)

(b)

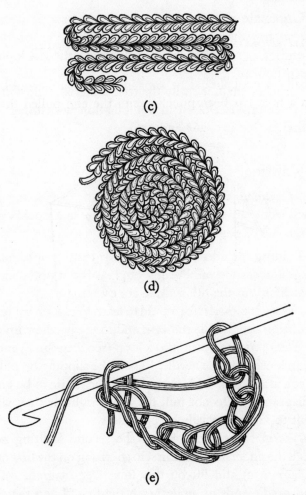

(c)

(d)

(e)

(see diagram a), so it cannot unravel accidentally. The basic stitch is the chain stitch, started with an ordinary slip knot and the loop pulled through and repeated (see diagram b). The stitch is identical to the chain stitch used for embroidery (see 268), except that here it is hooked rather than sewn (see diagram c).

The completed crochet chain can be coiled and sewn together in a variety of designs, round, square or hollow shaped (see diagrams c and d). At more advanced stages it can be crocheted together (see diagram e). Interweave or tie the loose end of a crocheted chain or design to the last loop that has been hooked.

The crochet chain is really the base material. The child can use it to improvise, often in combination with other knots and stitches (see 255, 268 and 276).

270 Knitting

Tools and materials: two knitting needles;
coloured wool yarn (wound in a ball and kept in a wool box; see diagram a on page 258)

Basic knitting includes four operations: casting on; knitting; purling; and casting off. Purling can be left out of the instructions at first, but the other three are essential.

Casting on: It is easiest for a child to learn to cast on using only one knitting needle. Tie the yarn end to the needle with a slip knot. Then twist the yarn into a loop (see diagram a) and slip the loop loosely on the needle. Repeat the slipping on of loops until you attain the width required for the fabric to be knitted (see diagram b). Do not pull the loops tight or they will be difficult to knit, especially by beginners.

Knit stitch: Pass the point of the second knitting needle through the underside of the first loop strung on the first needle (see diagram c) and lift off this loop (see diagram d). The second needle ends up underneath the first. Loop the excess yarn over the point of the second needle, back to front, as shown. Next, push the point of the second needle down close to the first, and lift the inner loop now formed on the first needle on to the second needle (see diagrams d and e). Repeat the series of operations until all loops have been lifted off the first needle and knitted on the second. Reverse the position of the needles in your hand and continue to knit as before.

Purl stitch: Cast the yarn on the first needle. Pick up the first

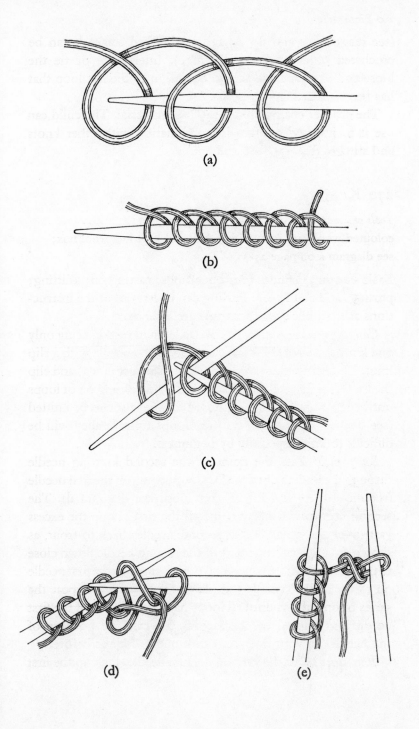

(a)

(b)

(c)

(d)

(e)

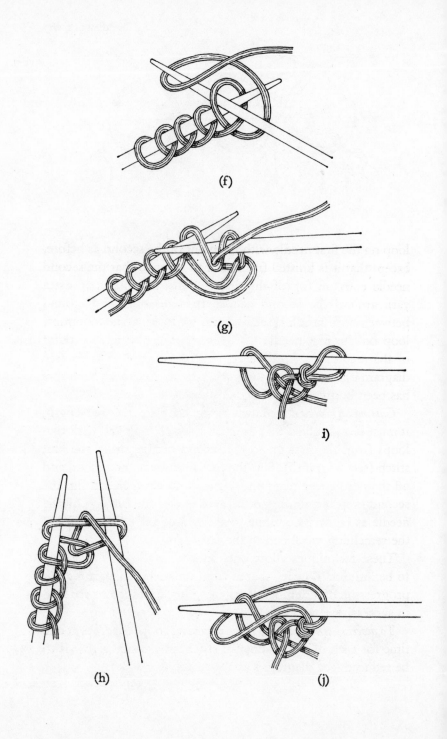

(f)

(g)

i)

(h)

(j)

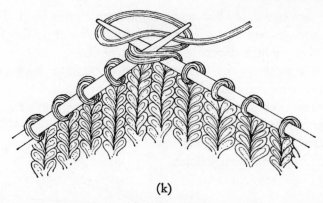

(k)

loop on the first needle with the point of the second as before, except that it is knitted from back to front so that the second needle ends on top of the first (see diagram f). Loop extra yarn around the second needle, front to back and around between both needles (see diagram g). Pick up the innermost loop on the first needle with the second, passing the point of the second up from below and lifting it off entirely (see diagram h). Continue to purl, reversing needles after each row has been knitted.

Casting off: When the fabric has reached the required length, it must be cast off so that the yarn does not unravel. Knit two loops from the first on to the second needle, using the knit stitch (see diagram i). Slip the first loop over the second and off the needle (see diagram j). Then knit another and slip the second loop remaining on the needle over the last and off the needle as before. Continue to the end of the row and tie off the remaining wool end to the last loop.

These techniques allow only square or rectangular shapes to be knitted. To vary shapes from the rectangular, a regular progression of a number of stitches must be added or reduced in successive rows.

To decrease stitches: Knit two successive loops together at one time for each of the number of stitches by which a row is to be reduced (see diagram k).

To increase stitches: Pick up one loop from the row just knitted and knit it into the next row for each of the number of stitches by which that row is to be increased.

Other methods for increasing and decreasing rows exist, but these are the simplest.

Different-coloured yarns used in various portions of a knit design allow the young craftsman to develop multicoloured patterns, cutting off the yarn used up to a point and tying on another of a different colour.

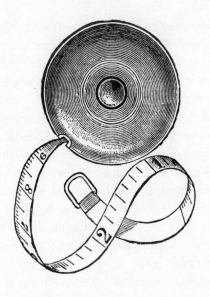

11 Fabric craft

The lif so short, the craft so long to lerne. *Geoffrey Chaucer*

271 Background

This chapter, like most of the others in this book, is not exhaustive. It concentrates on the development of a point of view and the beginning skills that can lead to more mature craftsmanship. The child's development follows that of the historic development of the various crafts themselves. The techniques for joining, fastening and binding cloth were primarily inherited from work with leather. The earliest clothing was mostly bound at the edges, laced and then draped, rather than sewn. Only the need to decorate, to make plain cloth more beautiful, inspired embroidery and stitching that ultimately led to more complex sewing. This in turn made it possible for woven cloth to be cut up in fitted patches which could be reassembled and sewn to follow the contour of the human figure and furniture. Inevitably this led to a need for a large variety of fine needles and other sewing implements and eventually to the sewing machine.

Sewing, other than hemming, was not widely practised in Europe until after the Crusades. But the needleworkers of the Orient and the ladies and their servants in European castles wove, embroidered and stitched decorative cloth for religious and regal ceremonies. Stitching and cloth-working skills served primarily to adorn royalty and nobility, as status symbols of wealth and power, and to enrich ritual. The techniques developed as playful and luxurious art forms before they were applied to everyday life.

Advanced sewing requires patterns. But it is a far cry from making such a pattern to merely following prefabricated patterns. Successful sewing of a garment depends on paper cutting, template making, and designing skills (see Chapter 2), not on just following an existing pattern. Without experience in inventing patterns, following printed patterns can be frustrating – and it results in ill-fitting garments.

To become familiar with the characteristics of cloth the child must first learn to explore and use the different kinds that are commonly available – wool, linen, cotton, velvet, silk and felt – as he would on being introduced to any other craft. He'll discover, for example, that fibres in all fabrics (except felt) unravel at the edges unless they are bound or hemmed. Hole-punching, lacing and binding, in cloth or in paper, give the child experience in joining one piece of material to the next. He needs exercise working in the flat as well as in working dimensionally in the round. He must start with relatively coarse thong or yarn until he can graduate to finer thread.

Cutting and pasting
272 Fabric pasting

Tools and materials: cardboard; fabric and felt scraps; scissors;
glue or paste (see 21–8)

When buying glue or paste, check the label to discover whether
it is suitable for fabric. Fabric adhesive should retain some
elasticity after it has dried completely. Cow gum is not
recommended.

Show the young child how to fold, hem and glue fabric
edges (other than felt) to avoid unravelling. All the suggestions
made for gluing paper apply (see 21–31, 88 and 125). (See also
165.)

273 Hole-punching and lacing

Tools and materials: same as 17–20, 126 and 127; fabric scraps

The same skills, tools and materials apply to cloth as to paper
and leather. Lacing through holes punched into the fabric
and binding it along the edges give the child a first insight
into sewing cloth.

274 Snap fastening

Tools and materials: same as 130; fabric scraps

Snap fasteners are easily attached to fabric by children old
enough to punch holes and handle a hammer. They can insert
the male and female of parts of each fastener into holes
punched into different or the same pieces of fabric and then
secure them with the die (see 130). An adult can do this for
younger children. Playing with snap fasteners, as with buttons
and buttonholes, helps a child learn to dress himself.

Sewing

275 Cutting fabric

Tools and materials: scissors or pinking shears; fabric

Cutting shapes out of fabric with scissors or pinking shears requires prior experience with paper. Start the child with relatively small cloth scraps. Show him that it is best to pin or tape smooth and wrinkle-free fabric to a large sheet of cardboard by one edge before trying to cut it. Hold the bottom edge firmly in hand while cutting. Rather than snipping with the point of the scissors, the child should try to cut fabric from the bottom of the cutting edges, where the scissors blades are joined.

276 Basic stitches

Tools and materials: fabric scraps; large sewing needle; coarse thread; thimble; pincushion

Show the child how to moisten and twist the end of the thread before trying to thread the sewing needle. Children who suffer vision or coordination defects should have this done for them. See 268 for basic stitches, which apply to sewing as to em-

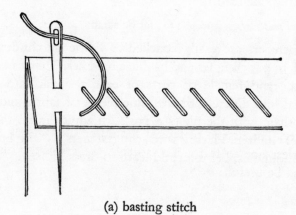

(a) basting stitch

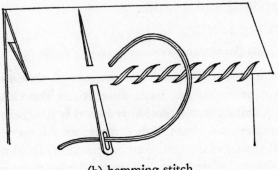

(b) hemming stitch

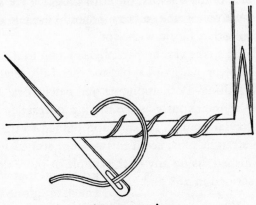

(c) oversewing

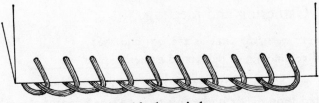

(d) blanket stitch

broidery. The first to be taught should be the running stitch, the easiest one to learn. The stitches shown in the diagram can also be useful.

277 Appliqué and quilting

Tools and materials: same as 268, 275 and 276;
backing fabric (linen, canvas or cotton)

Appliqué is essentially cloth collage, except that cut cloth shapes are sewn, rather than pasted, to a background. A running or back stitch (see 268) is easiest for beginners, but more complex and decorative stitches can be used by experienced young craftsmen. Assure that the child hems each piece of fabric before sewing it on the backing, so that the appliquéd shapes do not unravel at the edges. (See also 272.) Children in the youngest age groups should use felt shapes, or they can hem other fabric with tape.

An appliqué shape can be partially sewn on to the backing, stuffed with cotton wool or kapok, and then fully sewn to form patchwork quilting. Both appliqués and patchwork quilts can be designed spontaneously as the work progresses, or the cut shapes can be laid out in advance and pinned to the backing cloth with straight pins, sewn in position, stuffed if quilted, and then finished, using any of the simple or more decorative stitches described in 268 and 276.

278 Gathering and pleating

Tools and materials: same as 273, 275 and 276;
adhesive binding, or perforated gathering tape

It is easiest for beginners if they apply pre-punched or perforated binding or gathering tape to one edge of the fabric. By lacing through pre-cut holes children can form natural pleats. Or a child can punch holes into one edge of the fabric (see 273) after taping it with adhesive binding, or perforated gathering tape, and then lace and gather it. Pre-punched pleating tapes are available in needlework shops. The pleats can be left loosely gathered or the child can sew them partially or

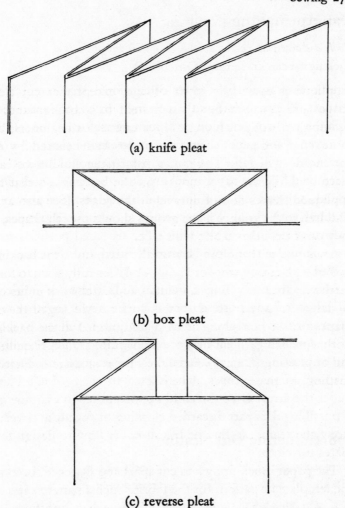

(a) knife pleat

(b) box pleat

(c) reverse pleat

fully, depending on the intended design or purpose (see diagram c). The three basic forms, knife, box and reverse pleats, can be gathered this way (see diagrams a–c, and the diagrams on page 44).

Pattern-making
279 Paper templates

Tools and materials: same as 63–5

Fabric that is to fit a three-dimensional shape requires a pattern. The shape around which the fabric is to be draped – a clothespeg doll, cushion or human figure – must be selected in advance and paper shapes cut to determine size and where the seams will fall. The paper pattern should be cut and assembled like the paper mock-up described in 64, and pieces added, snipped off or folded until they fit the shape to be covered with cloth. When completed, separate the mock-up so that it lies flat on the table. The flattened portions must later be cut out of cloth, hemmed, fitted and then sewn together.

Make sure the young craftsman adds widths of fabric on all edges of any portion that is to be sewn together with other portions, and along hems. Variations in fullness or shape of the finished garment may require tapering of edges, gathering or pleating (see 278). Armholes, for example, need special shaping so that sleeves, when sewn to them, don't bunch under the arms. Give the child opportunities to examine and if possible take apart discarded clothing or furniture covering along the seams, so that he can discover how to design templates for cloth.

The paper mock-up, when cut apart and flattened, becomes the template or pattern for the fabric. Such a pattern can consist of a single, flattened sheet which, when transferred to cloth, requires only folding over at seams and hems and sewing together, or of several individual shapes, each of which is hemmed separately and then sewn to the main body of the work.

280 Transfer from paper to cloth

Tools and materials: paper template or pattern (see 279);
straight pins; pincushion; tailor's chalk; cloth

Flatten the cloth on a tabletop and pin the paper pattern shapes
to it. Make sure that sufficient space is left between the shapes
for seams to be added where needed. Trace the edge of the
paper pattern on the cloth with tailor's chalk, adding a second
parallel line where an additional width for seams and hems is
required (see diagram). Keep the paper pattern pinned to the

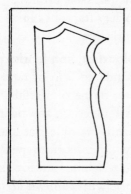

cloth until after it has been cut. Pleats can be indicated on the
paper pattern and then transferred to the cloth. Cover the
back of the paper pattern with a solid layer of chalk, pin it
again to the cloth, and trace the pleat lines marked on the
pattern with a ballpoint pen. They'll transfer to the cloth. Pin
the portions of traced pleats with straight pins wherever they
are to be sewn, after cutting the cloth, so that they can be
found and sewn later even if some of the chalk has rubbed off.

281 Sewing from a pattern

Tools and materials: same as 275 and 276

After the cloth has been cut and the paper pattern unpinned
from it, chalk the lines previously marked again to be sure

they will remain visible. Then sew along all marked seams, hems and pleats. Remind the child that all seams and hems must be sewn on the reverse side of the fabric and the final product turned over or inside out after it has been completed, so that the ragged cloth edges of seams and hems are hidden.

Decorating cloth
282 Painting on fabric

Tools and materials: textile paints and solvent; fabric;
bun tin for mixing colours; sable brushes;
cardboard mat, embroidery frame or canvas stretcher;
newspaper-covered worktable

Textile paints are colourfast, and fabrics painted or stencilled with them can be laundered. Pin or tape the fabric that is to be painted to the mat, frame or stretcher so that all surfaces to be decorated are stretched on top over the opening. Make sure the fabric surface is wrinkle-free and reasonably taut. It must not touch any other surface while being painted or before it has dried completely. Caution the child not to overload the brush or fabric with paint. A certain amount of crawl or bleeding of colours beyond the width of the brushstroke can be expected at times. Sections 136–9 and 153 apply to fabric painting, as to any other surface.

283 Stencilling and printing on fabric

Tools and materials: textile paints (for stencilling);
textile printing inks

See 205–8 for scrap materials printing; 214 and 215 for general printing instructions; 210 for cylinder printing; 211–13 for linoleum-block making and printing; 220 for stencil making and printing. All these processes apply to printing on fabric.

284 Dyeing

Commercial fabric dyes, like those used for leather, are highly toxic. They must be kept out of reach of small children, and even more mature ones should not be allowed to use them. However, young people can learn to make and use relatively non-toxic vegetable dyes. But note that even the most harmless dyes, due to their high concentration, can be irritating to the skin of some young people.

Before fabric can be dyed it must be treated with a mordant so that it is colourfast when dyed. The cautions about dyes apply to mordants too. Young people should wear rubber or plastic gloves, work in well-ventilated areas, and avoid inhaling the fumes from the boiling mordant and dye baths.

To prepare cloth for dyeing, the following are needed:

Tools and materials: copper or enamel pans, large enough so that the fabric to be dyed can be completely immersed and stirred in mordant and dye bath without spilling;
mordant (see below); dye (see below);
long-handled wooden spoon

Preparing wool for dyeing: Wash the fabric thoroughly in warm water and soap or detergent. Fill a pan with the required amount of water (see caution above) and bring to the boil. Add 25g (1 oz) of alum and 6g (¼oz) of cream of tartar for every 4 litres (gallon) of water. Immerse the fabric in the mordant and boil slowly for one hour. Stir the fabric with a wooden spoon to assure even saturation. Let the mixture and fabric cool until it can be handled safely, and then rinse the fabric thoroughly in cool water. Squeeze out excess moisture without twisting the wool and let dry overnight on a clothesline. Whether or not it is completely dry, the fabric will be ready for its dye bath next day.

Preparing cotton, linen or rayon fabrics for dyeing: Wash the fabric as above and boil the water. Add 25g (10z) of alum and 6g ($\frac{1}{4}$oz) of ordinary baking soda for every 4 litres (gallon) of water and proceed as with wool fabrics.

Preparing the dye bath: The following dyes can be made by boiling various plants, roots, nuts and berries until the solution reaches the desired colour intensity. Gather plants while they are young – roots in the autumn; leaves as soon as they are full grown; and berries, seeds and nuts when they have ripened.

Vegetable matter	Colour
Goldenrod (chop the whole plant into small segments and boil)	Yellow
Pear or peach tree leaves	Pale yellow
Black walnut husks and shells	Yellow-brown
Sunflower seeds and larkspur flowers	Blue
Beets	Violet
Dandelion roots	Dark pink

You can mix and dilute these to obtain other colours and shadings – blue and yellow make green, for example. Add the concentrated dye to a pan of gently boiling water. Be sure not to fill the pan more than enough to soak and cover the fabric (see caution above). Keep the pan boiling gently while the cloth is immersed and keep stirring with a wooden spoon until the fabric is dyed a colour of the desired intensity. Then remove with the spoon, rinse in clear running water, squeeze out the excess moisture gently, and hang with clothespegs from a line so that the cloth does not come into contact with itself or any other surface until it is completely dry.

285 Tie-dyeing

Tools and materials: fabric; mordant (see 284); dyes (see 284); thread or twine; steam iron and ironing board

Tie-dyeing is an ancient craft. Cloth is crumpled and tied into a ball, twisted into a spiral and tied, or folded and tied, or sewn temporarily so that, when immersed in a dye bath, the colour penetrates the fabric in certain places only. It is dyed according to the degree of penetration of the colour into the folds and creases of the wadded-together, tied or sewn fabric.

The illustrations show some of the methods of crumpling, twisting, folding, tying and sewing cloth for immersion in a dye bath (see diagram). The fabric must first be thoroughly washed and immersed in mordant and ironed, before it is prepared for the dye bath (see 284).

Index